SHIMBA
BIBLE STUDY SERIES

THE DIVINITY OF JESUS

IN THE BOOK OF COLOSSIANS

Dr. Maxwell Shimba

SHIMBA
PUBLISHING

TABLE OF CONTENTS

INTRODUCTION

The Supremacy of Christ in Colossians

The Book of Colossians stands as a monumental work in the New Testament, offering a rich tapestry of theological insights and practical teachings that are foundational to the Christian faith. Authored by the Apostle Paul, this epistle addresses the church in Colossae, a small city in Asia Minor. Despite its brevity, Colossians is profound in its scope, providing a comprehensive and exalted vision of Jesus Christ. Through its four chapters, Paul unveils the mysteries of Christ's divinity, His preeminent role in creation, and His ultimate authority as the sustainer and redeemer of all things.

Paul's primary aim in writing Colossians was to counteract false teachings that were infiltrating the church. These teachings, often referred to as the Colossian heresy, comprised elements of Jewish legalism, pagan mysticism, and early Gnostic thought, which collectively threatened to undermine the true gospel. Paul's response was to present a clear and compelling portrait of Christ that would dispel any confusion and fortify the believers' faith.

The Context of Colossians

To appreciate the depth of Paul's message, it's essential to understand the historical and cultural context of Colossae. The city was a melting pot of various religious and philosophical influences, which created a fertile ground for syncretism – the blending of different beliefs and practices. The church in Colossae, like many early Christian communities, was vulnerable to these external pressures.

Paul wrote this letter during his first imprisonment in Rome, around AD 60-62. Despite his physical confinement, Paul's spirit was not bound, and his concern for the churches he had nurtured continued to burn brightly. Epaphras, a fellow worker and likely the founder of the Colossian church, had brought news of the challenges facing the believers there, prompting Paul to address these issues head-on.

Key Themes of Colossians

The Book of Colossians can be summarized by several key themes that weave together to form a cohesive and powerful theological statement:

1. The Supremacy of Christ: Central to Colossians is the assertion of Christ's preeminence over all creation. Paul emphasizes that Jesus is not just another spiritual being or

enlightened teacher but the very image of the invisible God (Colossians 1:15). He is the firstborn over all creation, signifying His authority and priority in all things.

2. Christ as Creator and Sustainer: Paul vividly describes Jesus as the agent through whom all things were created, both in heaven and on earth, visible and invisible (Colossians 1:16). Not only did Jesus bring all things into existence, but He also sustains them, holding the universe together by His power (Colossians 1:17).

3. The Fullness of Deity in Christ: In Colossians 2:9, Paul declares that in Christ, all the fullness of the Deity lives in bodily form. This profound truth affirms the complete divinity of Jesus, who embodies all the attributes and essence of God.

4. Reconciliation Through Christ: Paul underscores the redemptive work of Jesus, who reconciled all things to Himself through His blood shed on the cross (Colossians 1:20). This reconciliation restores the broken relationship between humanity and God, offering peace and unity.

5. The Mystery of Christ: A recurring theme in Colossians is the revelation of the mystery hidden for ages but now disclosed to the saints – Christ in you, the hope of glory (Colossians 1:26-27). This mystery reveals the intimate and transformative presence of Christ within believers, providing a profound hope for the future.

6. Living a New Life in Christ: Paul exhorts the Colossians to live in a manner worthy of the Lord, setting their hearts on things above and putting to death their earthly nature (Colossians 3:1-5). The new life in Christ calls for a radical transformation in thought, behavior, and relationships.

The Relevance of Colossians Today

The teachings of Colossians are as relevant today as they were in the first century. In a world increasingly characterized by spiritual confusion and moral relativism, the clear and authoritative presentation of Jesus Christ in Colossians offers an anchor for our faith. The challenges faced by the Colossian church mirror those we encounter in contemporary society – competing ideologies, spiritual syncretism, and ethical dilemmas.

By immersing ourselves in the study of Colossians, we can fortify our understanding of who Jesus is and what He has accomplished. This epistle calls us to recognize Jesus' supremacy in every aspect of our lives, to embrace the fullness of His deity, and to live out the new identity we have in Him.

Overview of the Book

In the following chapters, we will journey through the Book of Colossians, unpacking its rich theological insights and practical applications. Each chapter will focus on specific lessons about Jesus, His divinity, and His work as Creator, Sustainer, and Author of our Salvation.

- Chapter 1: The Preeminence of Christ will explore Jesus' role as the image of God and the firstborn over all creation.

- Chapter 2: The Fullness of Deity in Christ will delve into the mystery of the incarnation and the completeness we find in Jesus.

- Chapter 3: New Life in Christ will discuss the transformative power of being raised with Christ and setting our minds on things above.

- Chapter 4: Christ, the Head of the Church will examine Jesus' leadership over the church and His resurrection power.

- Chapter 5: Reconciliation Through Christ will highlight the peace and restoration brought by Jesus' sacrificial death.

- Chapter 6: The Mystery of Christ in You will reflect on the hope and glory of Christ dwelling within believers.

Through this exploration, we will seek to deepen our understanding of Jesus' divinity and supremacy, allowing these truths to transform our faith and daily living. Join us on this journey as we uncover the profound lessons of Jesus in the Book of Colossians.

DR. MAXWELL SHIMBA

CHAPTER 01

THE PREEMINENCE OF CHRIST

The Eternal Sovereignty of Jesus

Key Verse: Colossians 1:15-18

Lesson: Jesus is the image of the invisible God, the firstborn over all creation. By Him, all things were created in heaven and on earth, visible and invisible. He is before all things, and in Him, all things hold together.

Colossians 1:15 using the NIV Bible.

"The Son is the image of the invisible God, the firstborn over all creation." (Colossians 1:15, NIV)

Interpretation:

This verse declares the preeminence and divinity of Jesus Christ. It affirms that Jesus is the visible representation of the invisible God and holds a position of supremacy over all creation, not as a created being, but as the one who has authority and preeminence over all things.

Commentary:

"The Son is the image of the invisible God":

- This statement identifies Jesus Christ as the perfect representation and manifestation of God, who is invisible. The term "image" (Greek: eikōn) indicates that Jesus perfectly reveals the nature, character, and essence of God. To see Jesus is to see God (John 14:9; Hebrews 1:3).

- Jesus is not merely a reflection of God but the exact representation of His being. This means that in Jesus, the fullness of God is present and visible to humanity, making the invisible God known (2 Corinthians 4:4).

"The firstborn over all creation":

- The term "firstborn" (Greek: prototokos) here refers to rank and preeminence rather than chronology. It emphasizes Jesus' supremacy and authority over all creation. In Jewish culture, the firstborn son had a place of honor and inheritance, which Paul uses metaphorically to express Christ's preeminence (Psalm 89:27).

- This does not imply that Jesus is a created being, but rather that He is the heir and ruler over all creation. He holds the highest position in the universe, being the one through whom and for whom all things were created (Colossians 1:16-17).

Concordance:

- Image of the invisible God: This phrase connects to the concept of Jesus being the exact representation of God, showing that in Christ, the invisible God is made visible (John 14:9; Hebrews 1:3).

- Firstborn over all creation: This term refers to Jesus' supremacy and authority, indicating His preeminence and rightful place as ruler over all creation (Psalm 89:27; Romans 8:29).

References from the NIV Bible:

1. John 14:9 (NIV): "Jesus answered: 'Don't you know me, Philip, even after I have been among you such a long time? Anyone who has seen me has seen the Father. How can you say, "Show us the Father"?'"

2. Hebrews 1:3 (NIV): "The Son is the radiance of God's glory and the exact representation of his being, sustaining all things by his powerful word. After he had provided purification for sins, he sat down at the right hand of the Majesty in heaven."

3. 2 Corinthians 4:4 (NIV): "The god of this age has blinded the minds of unbelievers, so that they cannot see the light of the gospel that displays the glory of Christ, who is the image of God."

4. Psalm 89:27 (NIV): "And I will appoint him to be my firstborn, the most exalted of the kings of the earth."

5. Colossians 1:16-17 (NIV): "For in him all things were created: things in heaven and on earth, visible and invisible, whether thrones or powers or rulers or authorities; all things have been created through him and for him. He is before all things, and in him all things hold together."

6. Romans 8:29 (NIV): "For those God foreknew he also predestined to be conformed to the image of his Son, that he might be the firstborn among many brothers and sisters."

Interpretation and Application:

- Christ's Divinity and Supremacy: This verse affirms the divine nature of Christ and His unique role in revealing God to humanity. Believers are encouraged to recognize Jesus as the fullest expression of God's character and to worship Him as Lord over all creation.

- Seeing God in Christ: For Christians, this verse is a powerful reminder that to know God, one must look to Jesus. In Christ, the character and purposes of God are fully revealed, making Him the ultimate source of spiritual truth and life.

- Christ's Authority: The concept of Jesus as the "firstborn" emphasizes His authority over all things. This calls believers to submit to His lordship, acknowledging Him as the ruler and sustainer of all creation.

Let's explore the theme of Christ's Divinity and Supremacy as highlighted in Colossians 1:15.

Christ's Divinity

1. The Image of the Invisible God:

- Exact Representation: The phrase "image of the invisible God" (Greek: eikōn) in Colossians 1:15 conveys that Jesus is not merely a reflection or likeness of God but is the exact and perfect representation of God's being. This is further emphasized in Hebrews 1:3, where Jesus is described as "the radiance of God's glory and the exact representation of his being." This means that everything about God—His nature, character, and attributes—is fully and perfectly revealed in Christ. Therefore, to see Jesus is to see God, as Jesus Himself said in John 14:9, "Anyone who has seen me has seen the Father."

- Revelation of the Invisible: In Jesus, the invisible God becomes visible to humanity. God, who is spirit and cannot be seen by human eyes, made Himself known and accessible through the incarnation of Christ. This is why Jesus is central to the Christian understanding of God; He is the full and complete revelation of who God is.

2. Divine Nature:

- Eternal Existence: The idea that Jesus is the image of the invisible God also affirms His eternal existence. Before anything was created, Christ existed with God and as God. This is consistent with John 1:1, which states, "In the beginning was the Word, and the Word was with God, and the Word was God." Therefore, Jesus is not a created being but has always existed as God.

- Divine Attributes: As the image of God, Jesus possesses all the attributes of God, including omnipotence, omniscience, and omnipresence. He exercises divine power, such as forgiving sins (Mark 2:5-7), calming storms (Mark 4:39), and raising the dead (John 11:43-44). These actions reveal that Jesus shares in the divine nature and authority of God Himself.

Christ's Supremacy

1. Firstborn Over All Creation:

- Preeminence in Rank: The term "firstborn" (Greek: prototokos) in this context refers not to birth order but to Christ's preeminence and supreme authority over all creation. In ancient cultures, the firstborn son held a place of honor and had the rights of inheritance. By calling Jesus the "firstborn," Paul is asserting that Jesus has the highest rank and authority over all that exists. This is supported by Psalm

89:27, where God says, "And I will appoint him to be my firstborn, the most exalted of the kings of the earth."

- Supreme Authority: As the firstborn, Jesus has authority over all creation, both seen and unseen. Colossians 1:16-17 expands on this by stating that "all things were created through him and for him" and that "in him all things hold together." Jesus is not just a part of creation; He is the agent through whom creation came into being and the one who sustains it. This supremacy means that Jesus is sovereign over the entire universe, including all spiritual and earthly powers.

2. Centrality in Redemption:

- Head of the Church: Christ's supremacy also extends to His role as the head of the Church. Colossians 1:18 states, "And he is the head of the body, the church; he is the beginning and the firstborn from among the dead, so that in everything he might have the supremacy." As the head, Jesus is the source of the Church's life and direction. His resurrection from the dead secures His place as the firstborn from the dead, ensuring that He is preeminent in all things, including the new creation.

- Universal Reconciliation: Through His death and resurrection, Jesus reconciles all things to God, making peace through His blood (Colossians 1:20). This act of redemption is the ultimate expression of His supremacy. It shows that

Jesus is not only supreme over creation but also over the redemption and restoration of all things. His work on the cross has universal implications, bringing everything in heaven and on earth under His lordship.

Application for Believers

- Worship and Adoration: Recognizing Christ's divinity and supremacy should lead believers to worship Him with reverence and awe. Jesus is not just a moral teacher or a prophet; He is God in the flesh, worthy of our highest honor and devotion.

- Submission to His Authority: Understanding Christ's supremacy means acknowledging His lordship over every aspect of our lives. Believers are called to submit to His authority, allowing Him to guide their thoughts, actions, and decisions.

- Confidence in His Sovereignty: Knowing that Jesus is supreme over all creation gives believers confidence and assurance, even in times of trouble. Because He holds all things together, we can trust that He is in control of our lives and the world around us.

Here's an expository study and comprehensive commentary on Colossians 1:16 using the New International Version (NIV) of the Bible.

"For in him all things were created: things in heaven and on earth, visible and invisible, whether thrones or powers or rulers or authorities; all things have been created through him and for him." (Colossians 1:16, NIV)

Interpretation:

In this verse, Paul emphasizes the preeminence of Christ in creation. He asserts that everything in existence—both in the physical and spiritual realms—was created by Christ, through Christ, and for Christ. This underscores Christ's supreme authority and His central role in the entire universe.

Commentary:

"For in him all things were created": Paul begins by affirming that Christ is the agent of all creation. Everything that exists finds its origin in Him. This statement reflects the divine nature of Christ, positioning Him as the Creator alongside God the Father (John 1:3; Hebrews 1:2).

"Things in heaven and on earth, visible and invisible": Paul expands on the scope of Christ's creative work, including everything in both the physical (earthly) and spiritual (heavenly) realms. This includes not just the material world but also the spiritual forces and entities (Ephesians 6:12).

"Whether thrones or powers or rulers or authorities": These terms refer to various levels and types of spiritual beings or angelic hierarchies. Paul asserts that Christ is above all these, having created them, thereby establishing His authority over all spiritual and cosmic powers (Ephesians 1:21; 1 Peter 3:22).

"All things have been created through him and for him": Not only were all things created by Christ, but they were also created for Him. This means that the purpose of all creation is ultimately to serve and glorify Christ. Everything exists for His glory and to fulfill His divine purpose (Romans 11:36; Revelation 4:11).

Concordance:

- For in him all things were created: This phrase asserts Christ as the Creator, reinforcing His divine nature and role in the origin of all things (John 1:3; Hebrews 1:2).

- Things in heaven and on earth, visible and invisible: This statement emphasizes the comprehensive scope of Christ's creation, encompassing both the physical and spiritual realms (Ephesians 6:12).

- Whether thrones or powers or rulers or authorities: These terms highlight the various levels of spiritual beings, all of which are subject to Christ's authority as their Creator (Ephesians 1:21; 1 Peter 3:22).

- All things have been created through him and for him: This phrase encapsulates the purpose and origin of all creation, affirming that everything exists to serve Christ's will and bring glory to Him (Romans 11:36; Revelation 4:11).

References from the New International Version (NIV):

1. John 1:3: "Through him all things were made; without him nothing was made that has been made."

2. Hebrews 1:2: "But in these last days he has spoken to us by his Son, whom he appointed heir of all things, and through whom also he made the universe."

3. Ephesians 6:12: "For our struggle is not against flesh and blood, but against the rulers, against the authorities, against the powers of this dark world and against the spiritual forces of evil in the heavenly realms."

4. Ephesians 1:21: "Far above all rule and authority, power and dominion, and every name that is invoked, not only in the present age but also in the one to come."

5. 1 Peter 3:22: "Who has gone into heaven and is at God's right hand—with angels, authorities and powers in submission to him."

6. Romans 11:36: "For from him and through him and for him are all things. To him be the glory forever! Amen."

7. Revelation 4:11: "You are worthy, our Lord and God, to receive glory and honor and power, for you created

all things, and by your will they were created and have their being."

Interpretation and Application:

- Christ as Creator: This verse highlights the essential role of Christ in creation, affirming His divine nature. Understanding Christ as the Creator helps believers recognize His authority over all things and His central role in the universe.

- Comprehensive Dominion: The inclusion of all realms—heavenly and earthly, visible and invisible—underlines the total dominion of Christ. This reinforces the idea that nothing exists outside His authority, offering comfort and assurance to believers who trust in His sovereign power.

- Purpose of Creation: The statement that all things were created "for Him" points to the ultimate purpose of all creation: to glorify Christ. This challenges believers to live in a way that aligns with this purpose, acknowledging Christ's lordship over every aspect of life.

Exploring Christ as Creator is foundational to understanding His divine nature and His role in the universe. This concept is deeply rooted in Christian theology and has significant implications for both doctrine and the believer's daily life.

Christ as Creator: Biblical Foundation

1. John 1:1-3 (NIV):

- "In the beginning was the Word, and the Word was with God, and the Word was God. He was with God in the beginning. Through him all things were made; without him nothing was made that has been made."

- Explanation: John begins his Gospel by identifying Jesus (the Word) as both divine and eternal, emphasizing that all creation came into existence through Him. This passage makes it clear that Christ is not a created being but is the agent of creation itself.

2. Hebrews 1:2 (NIV):

- "But in these last days he has spoken to us by his Son, whom he appointed heir of all things, and through whom also he made the universe."

- Explanation: This verse underscores that Christ is the one through whom God created the universe. It not only speaks to Christ's role in creation but also to His inheritance of all creation, establishing His authority over it.

3. Colossians 1:16 (NIV):

- "For in him all things were created: things in heaven and on earth, visible and invisible, whether thrones or powers or rulers or authorities; all things have been created through him and for him."

- Explanation: This verse, as discussed earlier, asserts Christ's comprehensive role in creation, including both the material and spiritual realms. It also highlights that creation exists for Him, indicating His ultimate purpose in creation.

Theological Implications of Christ as Creator

1. Christ's Divinity and Preexistence:

- The role of Christ in creation affirms His divine nature and eternal existence. Since all things were made through Him, Christ must be uncreated and eternal, existing before all things. This aligns with the Christian doctrine of the Trinity, where Christ (the Son) is fully God, co-eternal with the Father and the Holy Spirit.

- John 8:58 (NIV): "Very truly I tell you," Jesus answered, "before Abraham was born, I am!" This statement by Jesus reinforces His preexistence and divine identity, echoing God's self-revelation in the Old Testament (Exodus 3:14).

2. Christ's Sovereignty Over Creation:

- As the Creator, Christ has absolute authority over all creation. This includes not only the physical world but also the spiritual realm, including all powers and authorities. Understanding Christ as the sovereign Creator reinforces the belief that nothing in creation is outside of His control or influence.

- Matthew 28:18 (NIV): "Then Jesus came to them and said, 'All authority in heaven and on earth has been given to me.'" This verse highlights the comprehensive authority Christ holds, a natural extension of His role as Creator.

3. Purpose and Meaning in Creation:

- The statement that all things were created "through Him and for Him" (Colossians 1:16) suggests that Christ is both the source and the goal of all creation. This means that the purpose of the universe, including humanity, is to fulfill the will and glorify the person of Christ.

- Romans 11:36 (NIV): "For from him and through him and for him are all things. To him be the glory forever! Amen." This verse encapsulates the idea that Christ is the ultimate purpose behind all existence, which calls believers to live in a way that glorifies Him.

4. Redemption and New Creation:

- Christ's role as Creator ties directly into His work in redemption. Just as He brought the original creation into existence, Christ also brings about a new creation through His redemptive work on the cross. Believers are considered "new creations" in Christ, a concept that reflects the ongoing work of Christ as Creator in restoring and renewing all things.

- 2 Corinthians 5:17 (NIV): "Therefore, if anyone is in Christ, the new creation has come: The old has gone, the new is here!" This speaks to the transformative power of Christ's creative and redemptive work in the lives of believers.

5. Christ's Role in Sustaining Creation:

- Christ is not only the Creator but also the sustainer of all things. The ongoing existence and order of the universe depend on His continual involvement. This aspect of Christ's work highlights His intimate connection with creation and His ongoing care for it.

- Hebrews 1:3 (NIV): "The Son is the radiance of God's glory and the exact representation of his being, sustaining all things by his powerful word." This passage emphasizes Christ's active role in sustaining the universe, underscoring His continual sovereignty and care.

Practical Implications for Believers

1. Worship and Reverence:

- Understanding Christ as Creator should inspire deep worship and reverence. Recognizing that the one who created the universe is also the one who died for humanity elevates the significance of His sacrifice and His love.

- Revelation 4:11 (NIV): "You are worthy, our Lord and God, to receive glory and honor and power, for you created all things, and by your will they were created and have their being."

2. Trust and Confidence:

- Believers can have confidence in Christ's authority over all aspects of life. Knowing that He is the Creator and sustainer of all things provides assurance that nothing is beyond His control, even in the midst of life's challenges.

- Colossians 1:17 (NIV): "He is before all things, and in him all things hold together." This verse reassures believers that Christ holds all creation together, including their own lives.

3. Purpose and Direction:

- Since all things were created for Christ, believers are called to live lives that align with this purpose. This means living in a way that glorifies Christ and fulfills His will, understanding that their ultimate purpose is found in Him.

- Ephesians 2:10 (NIV): "For we are God's handiwork, created in Christ Jesus to do good works, which God prepared in advance for us to do." This verse highlights the purpose of believers as part of God's creation, called to live out good works that reflect His glory.

Understanding Christ as Creator is foundational to Christian belief, shaping how believers view the world, their purpose, and their relationship with God. It reinforces

Christ's divinity, sovereignty, and ongoing role in the universe, providing a basis for worship, trust, and purposeful living. Recognizing Christ as the Creator calls believers to a life of reverence, obedience, and alignment with His will, knowing that their ultimate purpose is to glorify Him in all things.

Here's an expository study and comprehensive commentary on Colossians 1:17 using the New International Version (NIV) Bible.

"He is before all things, and in him all things hold together." (Colossians 1:17, NIV)

Interpretation:

In this verse, Paul emphasizes the preeminence and sustaining power of Christ. He asserts that Christ existed before all creation and that it is through Him that the entire universe is sustained and held together.

Commentary:

"He is before all things": This phrase underscores the eternal nature of Christ. "Before all things" indicates that Christ existed before anything was created, affirming His pre-existence and divine nature. This aligns with John 1:1-3, where Christ (the Word) is described as being with God in the beginning and through whom all things were made. Christ's existence before creation highlights His supremacy over all creation.

"And in him all things hold together": This statement reveals Christ's role in sustaining the universe. Not only did Christ create all things, but He also continues to sustain them. The phrase "hold together" suggests that Christ is the cohesive force that maintains the order and coherence of the universe. Without Christ, the entire creation would fall into chaos. This aligns with Hebrews 1:3, where Christ is described as sustaining all things by His powerful word.

Concordance:

- "He is before all things": This phrase relates to the concept of Christ's pre-existence and His eternal nature, affirming that He existed before the creation of the world (John 1:1-3; Revelation 22:13).

- "In him all things hold together": This phrase indicates Christ's role as the sustainer of the universe, emphasizing that He maintains the order and coherence of creation (Hebrews 1:3; Acts 17:28).

References from the NIV Bible:

1. John 1:1-3 (NIV): "In the beginning was the Word, and the Word was with God, and the Word was God. He was with God in the beginning. Through him all things were made; without him nothing was made that has been made."

2. Hebrews 1:3 (NIV): "The Son is the radiance of God's glory and the exact representation of his being,

sustaining all things by his powerful word. After he had provided purification for sins, he sat down at the right hand of the Majesty in heaven."

3. Revelation 22:13 (NIV): "I am the Alpha and the Omega, the First and the Last, the Beginning and the End."

4. Acts 17:28 (NIV): "For in him we live and move and have our being. As some of your own poets have said, 'We are his offspring.'"

Interpretation and Application:

- Christ's Preeminence: This verse teaches the preeminence of Christ in all things. As the One who existed before all creation and as the sustainer of the universe, Christ holds the highest place of honor and authority. This challenges believers to acknowledge Christ's supremacy in every aspect of their lives.

- Dependence on Christ: The fact that "in him all things hold together" emphasizes the ongoing dependence of creation on Christ. It reminds believers that everything in the universe, including their own lives, is sustained by Christ's power. This understanding should lead to a deeper trust in Christ's ability to sustain and guide them through life's challenges.

- Unity and Order in Christ: The phrase "hold together" also speaks to the unity and order that Christ brings to creation. In a world that often seems chaotic, this truth reassures believers that Christ is the ultimate source of stability and coherence.

Let's delve deeper into the concept of Christ's Preeminence as highlighted in Colossians 1:17.

Christ's Preeminence Explained

Preeminence refers to being first in rank, authority, and importance. In Christian theology, Christ's preeminence is the doctrine that Jesus Christ holds the supreme position over all creation, both in heaven and on earth. This preeminence is multifaceted, encompassing His role in creation, His sustaining power, His authority in the Church, and His ultimate purpose in the redemption of humanity.

1. Preeminence in Creation

- Colossians 1:16-17 (NIV) says, "For in him all things were created: things in heaven and on earth, visible and invisible, whether thrones or powers or rulers or authorities; all things have been created through him and for him. He is before all things, and in him all things hold together."

- Christ is not a part of creation; rather, He is the Creator. This means that He is before all things in both time and status. All things were made through Him, and nothing in existence came into being without Him. This affirms His divine nature and eternal existence. The universe exists because of Him, through Him, and for Him.

2. Preeminence in Sustaining All Things

- As Colossians 1:17 indicates, "in him all things hold together." This means that Christ is not only the Creator but also the Sustainer of everything. The cosmos continues to function, and every element within it remains in its proper order due to Christ's sustaining power.

- Hebrews 1:3 (NIV) echoes this, stating that Christ is "sustaining all things by his powerful word." This ongoing act of sustaining creation underscores His continuous involvement with His creation and His omnipotence.

3. Preeminence in the Church

- Colossians 1:18 (NIV) adds, "And he is the head of the body, the church; he is the beginning and the firstborn from among the dead, so that in everything he might have the supremacy."

- Christ's preeminence is also reflected in His relationship with the Church. As the head of the Church, Christ holds the highest authority and guides the Church in all its endeavors. His resurrection ("firstborn from among the dead") also signifies His victory over death and His role as the source of eternal life for believers.

4. Preeminence in Redemption

- Christ's preeminence is central to His work of redemption. Through His death and resurrection, He reconciled all things to Himself, making peace through His blood shed on the cross (Colossians 1:19-20). This act of redemption is the ultimate demonstration of His supremacy, as it fulfills God's plan of salvation for humanity.

5. Preeminence in the Future

- Christ's preeminence extends into the future as He will be recognized by all creation as Lord. Philippians 2:9-11 (NIV) states, "Therefore God exalted him to the highest place and gave him the name that is above every name, that at the name of Jesus every knee should bow, in heaven and on earth and under the earth, and every tongue acknowledge that Jesus Christ is Lord, to the glory of God the Father."

- This passage speaks to the future acknowledgment of Christ's supremacy by all of creation, further establishing His preeminence in all things.

Implications of Christ's Preeminence for Believers

1. Worship: Recognizing Christ's preeminence should lead believers to a deeper sense of worship and adoration. As the supreme Creator and Sustainer, He deserves our highest praise and devotion.

2. Trust: Understanding that Christ sustains all things provides a foundation for trust. Believers can rest in the

knowledge that Christ is in control of the universe and their lives.

3. Obedience: As the head of the Church and the supreme authority, Christ's preeminence calls for submission and obedience. Believers are to follow His guidance and commandments, acknowledging His rightful place as Lord over their lives.

4. Unity: In the Church, Christ's preeminence serves as the basis for unity. All members of the body of Christ are united under His lordship, which should foster harmony and mutual respect within the Church.

5. Mission: Christ's preeminence in redemption and His future return motivate believers to share the gospel. As the One who holds all authority, Christ's command to make disciples (Matthew 28:18-20) is to be taken seriously.

Christ's preeminence is a foundational doctrine that impacts every aspect of Christian faith and life. It reminds believers of Christ's ultimate authority, His ongoing involvement in the world, and His central role in the salvation of humanity. Recognizing and responding to Christ's preeminence is essential for a vibrant and faithful Christian walk.

Here's an expository study and comprehensive commentary on Colossians 1:18 using the NIV Bible.

"And he is the head of the body, the church; he is the beginning and the firstborn from among the dead, so that in everything he might have the supremacy." (Colossians 1:18, NIV)

Interpretation:

In this verse, Paul highlights the preeminence of Christ in both the church and creation. He emphasizes Christ's role as the head of the church, His resurrection as the "firstborn from among the dead," and His ultimate supremacy in all things.

Commentary:

"And he is the head of the body, the church":

- Christ is described as the "head" of the church, which is metaphorically referred to as "the body." This imagery underscores Christ's authority, leadership, and intimate connection with the church. As the head, Christ directs and sustains the church, guiding it according to His will (Ephesians 1:22-23; 1 Corinthians 12:27).

"He is the beginning":

- This phrase indicates that Christ is the source and origin of all creation. "Beginning" can also be understood as the "author" or "pioneer." It highlights His role in creation and the new creation through His resurrection (Revelation 3:14; John 1:1-3).

"And the firstborn from among the dead":

- The term "firstborn" here does not mean that Christ was the first to be raised from the dead chronologically but rather that He holds the highest rank among those resurrected. His resurrection is the guarantee of the future resurrection of all believers. This title also points to Christ's authority over death and His role in inaugurating the new creation (1 Corinthians 15:20; Revelation 1:5).

"So that in everything he might have the supremacy":

- This statement encapsulates the main point of the verse: Christ's supremacy in all things. Whether in creation, the church, or resurrection, Christ is supreme. This reflects His ultimate authority and preeminence over all powers and dominions (Philippians 2:9-11; Ephesians 1:20-23).

Concordance:

- Head of the body, the church: This phrase is central to Paul's ecclesiology, depicting Christ's authority and the church's dependence on Him (Ephesians 5:23; 1 Corinthians 12:12-27).

- The beginning: This term reflects Christ's role as the origin and source of all things, particularly in the context of creation and resurrection (John 1:1-3; Revelation 22:13).

- Firstborn from among the dead: This title emphasizes Christ's resurrection and preeminence in the new creation, being the first to rise in a glorified body and the leader of those who will follow (Romans 8:29; 1 Corinthians 15:20).

- Supremacy: This concept highlights Christ's ultimate authority over all creation, both visible and invisible, affirming His divine sovereignty (Philippians 2:9-11; Ephesians 1:20-23).

References from the NIV Bible:

1. Ephesians 1:22-23 (NIV): "And God placed all things under his feet and appointed him to be head over everything for the church, which is his body, the fullness of him who fills everything in every way."

2. 1 Corinthians 12:27 (NIV): "Now you are the body of Christ, and each one of you is a part of it."

3. Revelation 3:14 (NIV): "To the angel of the church in Laodicea write: These are the words of the Amen, the faithful and true witness, the ruler of God's creation."

4. 1 Corinthians 15:20 (NIV): "But Christ has indeed been raised from the dead, the firstfruits of those who have fallen asleep."

5. Philippians 2:9-11 (NIV): "Therefore God exalted him to the highest place and gave him the name that is above every name, that at the name of Jesus every knee should bow, in heaven and on earth and under the earth, and every tongue

acknowledge that Jesus Christ is Lord, to the glory of God the Father."

6. Ephesians 5:23 (NIV): "For the husband is the head of the wife as Christ is the head of the church, his body, of which he is the Savior."

Interpretation and Application:

- Christ's Authority and Leadership: As the head of the church, Christ's leadership and authority are paramount. Believers are called to recognize and submit to His authority in every aspect of life and within the church.

- Christ's Resurrection: The reference to Christ as the "firstborn from among the dead" underscores the importance of the resurrection in Christian faith. Christ's resurrection is the foundation of hope for all believers, assuring them of their future resurrection and eternal life.

- Christ's Supremacy: The emphasis on Christ's supremacy in all things challenges believers to view Him as preeminent in their lives. This calls for a life of worship, obedience, and allegiance to Christ above all else.

The Eternal Sovereignty of Jesus as Exhibited in the Book of Revelation

Introduction

The eternal sovereignty of Jesus Christ is a central theme in Christian theology, affirming His supreme authority and reign over all creation. This sovereignty is not only established in the Gospels and Epistles but is also powerfully illustrated in the Book of Revelation. In this chapter, we will explore the eternal sovereignty of Jesus as exhibited in Revelation, where He is depicted as the reigning King, the Alpha and Omega, and the ultimate judge of all things.

The Vision of the Glorified Christ

Key Verses: Revelation 1:12-18

John's vision of the glorified Christ at the beginning of Revelation provides a profound image of Jesus' eternal sovereignty. Here, Jesus is depicted in His divine glory, standing among seven golden lampstands, representing the seven churches.

- Revelation 1:12-13 (NIV): "I turned around to see the voice that was speaking to me. And when I turned I saw seven golden lampstands, and among the lampstands was someone like a son of man, dressed in a robe reaching down to his feet and with a golden sash around his chest."

Expository Insights:

- Seven Golden Lampstands (Strong's G3087): Represent the seven churches, indicating Christ's presence among His people.

- Son of Man (Strong's G5207 and G444): A title emphasizing Jesus' humanity and divinity, echoing the Messianic vision in Daniel 7:13-14.

In this passage, Jesus is further described as holding seven stars in His right hand, a symbol of His authority over the church. His face shines with the brilliance of the sun, underscoring His divine nature and eternal power.

- Revelation 1:17-18 (NIV): "When I saw him, I fell at his feet as though dead. Then he placed his right hand on me and said: 'Do not be afraid. I am the First and the Last. I am the Living One; I was dead, and now look, I am alive for ever and ever! And I hold the keys of death and Hades.'"

Here, Jesus declares Himself as the "First and the Last," affirming His eternal existence and sovereign authority over life and death. This vision sets the stage for the rest of Revelation, where Jesus' sovereignty is further revealed through His judgments, reign, and ultimate victory.

Jesus, the Alpha and the Omega

Key Verses: Revelation 22:12-13

Throughout Revelation, Jesus is repeatedly referred to as the Alpha and the Omega, the beginning and the end, emphasizing His eternal sovereignty over all creation.

- Revelation 22:12-13 (NIV): "Look, I am coming soon! My reward is with me, and I will give to each person according to what they have done. I am the Alpha and the Omega, the First and the Last, the Beginning and the End."

Expository Insights:

- Alpha and Omega (Strong's G1 and G5598): Represent the first and last letters of the Greek alphabet, symbolizing Jesus' comprehensive authority over all time and creation.

- Beginning and End (Strong's G746 and G5056): Emphasize Jesus as the origin and consummation of all things, affirming His role in creation and His sovereign control over its destiny.

This declaration highlights Jesus' role as the eternal sovereign who presides over history, guiding it toward its ultimate fulfillment in God's plan. His sovereignty encompasses all of time and space, ensuring that everything will culminate according to His divine will.

The Lamb Who Was Slain and the Sovereign Judge

Key Verses: Revelation 5:6-10

In Revelation, Jesus is also depicted as the Lamb who was slain, a powerful image that combines His sacrificial role with His sovereign authority. In chapter 5, the Lamb is the only one found worthy to open the scroll, symbolizing His authority to execute God's plan of redemption and judgment.

- Revelation 5:6-7 (NIV): "Then I saw a Lamb, looking as if it had been slain, standing at the center of the throne, encircled by the four living creatures and the elders. The Lamb had seven horns and seven eyes, which are the seven spirits of God sent out into all the earth. He went and took the scroll from the right hand of him who sat on the throne."

Expository Insights:

- Lamb (Strong's G721): Represents Jesus' sacrificial death, emphasizing His role as the Redeemer.

- Seven Horns and Seven Eyes (Strong's G2768 and G3788): Symbolize complete power (horns) and perfect knowledge (eyes), reflecting Jesus' omnipotence and omniscience.

The response of the heavenly beings to the Lamb further emphasizes His sovereignty:

- Revelation 5:9-10 (NIV): "And they sang a new song, saying: 'You are worthy to take the scroll and to open its seals, because you were slain, and with your blood you purchased for God persons from every tribe and language and people and nation. You have made them to be a kingdom and priests to serve our God, and they will reign on the earth.'"

This passage underscores that Jesus' sovereignty is rooted in His sacrificial death, which redeemed humanity and established His authority to judge and reign over the earth.

The Rider on the White Horse

Key Verses: Revelation 19:11-16

In Revelation 19, Jesus is portrayed as a mighty warrior and righteous judge, riding on a white horse to execute judgment and establish His reign.

- Revelation 19:11-13 (NIV): "I saw heaven standing open and there before me was a white horse, whose rider is called Faithful and True. With justice he judges and wages war. His eyes are like blazing fire, and on his head are many crowns. He has a name written on him that no one knows but he himself. He is dressed in a robe dipped in blood, and his name is the Word of God."

Expository Insights:

- White Horse (Strong's G3022): Symbolizes victory and purity.

- Many Crowns (Strong's G1238): Represent Jesus' supreme authority over all kingdoms.

- Word of God (Strong's G3056): Highlights Jesus as the divine Logos, the ultimate revelation of God.

This vision culminates with Jesus being recognized as "King of kings and Lord of lords," a title that affirms His supreme authority over all earthly and spiritual powers.

- Revelation 19:16 (NIV): "On his robe and on his thigh he has this name written: KING OF KINGS AND LORD OF LORDS."

This depiction of Jesus as the triumphant warrior and sovereign judge reinforces His eternal sovereignty and the certainty of His ultimate victory over evil.

The New Heaven and the New Earth

Key Verses: Revelation 21:1-7

The final chapters of Revelation present the fulfillment of Jesus' sovereign reign in the creation of a new heaven and a new earth. In this renewed creation, Jesus' sovereignty is fully realized as He dwells with His people in eternal peace and glory.

- Revelation 21:1-3 (NIV): "Then I saw 'a new heaven and a new earth,' for the first heaven and the first earth had passed away, and there was no longer any sea. I saw the Holy City, the new Jerusalem, coming down out of heaven from God, prepared as a bride beautifully dressed for her husband. And I heard a loud voice from the throne saying, 'Look! God's dwelling place is now among the people, and he will dwell with them. They will be his people, and God himself will be with them and be their God.'"

Expository Insights:

- New Heaven and New Earth (Strong's G2537 and G1093): Symbolize the complete renewal of creation under Jesus' sovereign rule.

- New Jerusalem (Strong's G2419): Represents the redeemed community, fully united with God.

In this vision, Jesus' eternal sovereignty is fully manifested as He reigns over a renewed and perfected creation, where sin, death, and suffering are no more.

- Revelation 21:6-7 (NIV): "He said to me: 'It is done. I am the Alpha and the Omega, the Beginning and the End. To the thirsty I will give water without cost from the spring of the water of life. Those who are victorious will inherit all this, and I will be their God and they will be my children.'"

This passage concludes the narrative of Revelation by affirming that Jesus' eternal sovereignty ensures the ultimate restoration and fulfillment of God's plan for humanity and the world.

Conclusion

The Book of Revelation presents a powerful and compelling portrayal of Jesus' eternal sovereignty. From the vision of the glorified Christ to the depiction of the Lamb who was slain, and from the rider on the white horse to the new heaven and new earth, Revelation affirms that Jesus is the supreme ruler over all creation. His sovereignty is eternal, encompassing all time and space, and His authority is unchallenged. For believers, this truth provides profound assurance and hope, knowing that Jesus, the Alpha and Omega, holds all things together and will ultimately bring about the fulfillment of God's perfect plan in the new creation.

Jesus as the Image of God

Key Verse: Colossians 1:15-18

Lesson: Jesus is the image of the invisible God, the firstborn over all creation. By Him, all things were created in heaven and on earth, visible and invisible. He is before all things, and in Him, all things hold together.

Jesus as the Image of God: An Expository Study in the Book of Revelation

Introduction

The concept of Jesus as the image of God is central to Christian theology. In the New Testament, this theme is powerfully depicted not only in Paul's letters but also in the Book of Revelation. The imagery and visions in Revelation provide a profound insight into the nature and character of Jesus as the perfect representation of God. This chapter will explore Jesus as the image of God as exhibited in Revelation, using an expository study method with references from Strong's Concordance to deepen our understanding.

The Radiant Glory of Christ

Key Verse: Revelation 1:12-16

The opening vision of Jesus in Revelation sets the stage for understanding His divine nature and glory. John's description of the risen Christ is rich with symbolism that points to His identity as the image of God.

- Revelation 1:12-16 (NIV): "I turned around to see the voice that was speaking to me. And when I turned I saw seven golden lampstands, and among the lampstands was someone like a son of man, dressed in a robe reaching down to his feet and with a golden sash around his chest. The hair on his head was white like wool, as white as snow, and his eyes were like blazing fire. His feet were like bronze glowing in a furnace, and his voice was like the sound of rushing waters. In his right hand he held seven stars, and coming out of his mouth was a sharp, double-edged sword. His face was like the sun shining in all its brilliance."

Expository Insights:

- Seven Golden Lampstands (Strong's G3087): Represent the seven churches, indicating Jesus' intimate presence and oversight among His people.

- Son of Man (Strong's G5207 and G444): A title that connects Jesus to Daniel's vision (Daniel 7:13-14), emphasizing His messianic role and divine authority.

- White Hair (Strong's G3022): Symbolizes purity, holiness, and eternal wisdom, reflecting the ancient of days (Daniel 7:9).

- Blazing Eyes (Strong's G3788): Denote His penetrating vision and omniscience, capable of seeing into the hearts and minds of all.

- Glowing Feet (Strong's G5474): Represent judgment and strength, signifying His authority and stability.

- Voice Like Rushing Waters (Strong's G5456): Emphasizes the power and majesty of His word, commanding attention and obedience.

- Double-edged Sword (Strong's G4501): Symbolizes the penetrating and discerning nature of His word, which judges the thoughts and attitudes of the heart.

- Face Like the Sun (Strong's G2246): Reflects His divine glory and brilliance, echoing the transfiguration (Matthew 17:2) and His exalted status.

The Throne Room Vision

Key Verse: Revelation 4:2-11

In Revelation 4, John is given a vision of the heavenly throne room, where the majesty and sovereignty of God are displayed. Jesus, as the Lamb, is central to this vision, symbolizing His sacrificial role and divine nature.

- Revelation 4:2-3 (NIV): "At once I was in the Spirit, and there before me was a throne in heaven with someone sitting on it. And the one who sat there had the appearance of jasper and ruby. A rainbow that shone like an emerald encircled the throne."

Expository Insights:

- Throne in Heaven (Strong's G2362): Represents God's sovereign rule and authority over all creation.

- Appearance of Jasper and Ruby (Strong's G2393 and G4556): Symbolize God's glory, purity, and righteous judgment.

- Emerald Rainbow (Strong's G2463): Signifies God's covenant faithfulness and mercy.

The Worthy Lamb

Key Verse: Revelation 5:6-14

Revelation 5 introduces Jesus as the Lamb who was slain, underscoring His redemptive work and His worthiness to open the scroll and execute God's plan.

- Revelation 5:6 (NIV): "Then I saw a Lamb, looking as if it had been slain, standing at the center of the throne, encircled by the four living creatures and the elders. The Lamb had seven horns and seven eyes, which are the seven spirits of God sent out into all the earth."

Expository Insights:

- Lamb (Strong's G721): Represents Jesus as the sacrificial Lamb of God, highlighting His atoning death (John 1:29).

- Seven Horns (Strong's G2768): Symbolize complete power and authority.

- Seven Eyes (Strong's G3788): Represent perfect knowledge and the fullness of the Holy Spirit (Isaiah 11:2).

The King of Kings and Lord of Lords

Key Verses: Revelation 19:11-16

In Revelation 19, Jesus is depicted as the victorious King of Kings and Lord of Lords, leading the heavenly armies to triumph over evil.

- Revelation 19:11-16 (NIV): "I saw heaven standing open and there before me was a white horse, whose rider is called Faithful and True. With justice he judges and wages war. His eyes are like blazing fire, and on his head are many crowns. He has a name written on him that no one knows but he himself. He is dressed in a robe dipped in blood, and his name is the Word of God. The armies of heaven were following him, riding on white horses and dressed in fine linen, white and clean. Coming out of his mouth is a sharp sword with which to strike down the nations. 'He will rule them with an iron scepter.' He treads the winepress of the fury of the wrath of God Almighty. On his robe and on his thigh he has this name written: KING OF KINGS AND LORD OF LORDS."

Expository Insights:

- White Horse (Strong's G3022): Symbolizes victory and purity.

- Faithful and True (Strong's G4103 and G228): Titles that emphasize Jesus' reliability and integrity.

- Many Crowns (Strong's G1238): Represent His supreme authority over all earthly and heavenly realms.

- Word of God (Strong's G3056): Highlights Jesus' role as the divine Logos, the ultimate revelation of God (John 1:1).

- Iron Scepter (Strong's G4464): Symbolizes His unyielding rule and judgment (Psalm 2:9).

The New Heaven and the New Earth

Key Verses: Revelation 21:1-7

The final chapters of Revelation describe the establishment of a new heaven and a new earth, where Jesus reigns eternally with His people, underscoring His role as the perfect image of God.

- Revelation 21:1-4 (NIV): "Then I saw 'a new heaven and a new earth,' for the first heaven and the first earth had passed away, and there was no longer any sea. I saw the Holy City, the new Jerusalem, coming down out of heaven from

God, prepared as a bride beautifully dressed for her husband. And I heard a loud voice from the throne saying, 'Look! God's dwelling place is now among the people, and he will dwell with them. They will be his people, and God himself will be with them and be their God. He will wipe every tear from their eyes. There will be no more death or mourning or crying or pain, for the old order of things has passed away.'"

Expository Insights:

- New Heaven and New Earth (Strong's G2537 and G1093): Symbolize the complete renewal and restoration of creation.

- New Jerusalem (Strong's G2419): Represents the redeemed community of God's people.

- God's Dwelling with Humanity (Strong's G4637): Emphasizes the intimate and eternal relationship between God and His people.

- The elimination of death, mourning, crying, and pain signifies the ultimate victory of Jesus over all forms of evil and suffering.

The Book of Revelation provides a majestic and awe-inspiring depiction of Jesus Christ as the image of God. From the radiant glory of His appearance in the opening vision to His role as the worthy Lamb and the triumphant King of Kings, Jesus embodies the fullness of God's nature and character. These vivid images and powerful declarations offer hope and assurance to believers, reminding us of the ultimate victory of Christ and the fulfillment of God's redemptive plan. As we reflect on these truths, may we be encouraged to live faithfully under the lordship of Jesus, the perfect image of God.

Jesus as Creator

Key Verse: Colossians 1:15-18

Lesson: Jesus is the image of the invisible God, the firstborn over all creation. By Him, all things were created in heaven and on earth, visible and invisible. He is before all things, and in Him, all things hold together.

Jesus as Creator: An Expository Study in the Book of Revelation

Introduction

The theme of Jesus as Creator is central to Christian theology and is vividly depicted in the Book of Revelation. This chapter will explore the implications of Jesus being the agent of creation, examining how this foundational truth shapes our understanding of the universe and our place within it. Through an expository study method and references from Strong's Concordance, we will delve into the rich imagery and declarations in Revelation that underscore Jesus' role as Creator.

The Proclamation of Jesus as Creator

Key Verses: Revelation 3:14, 4:11

Revelation explicitly acknowledges Jesus as the source of all creation, affirming His preeminence and authority over everything that exists.

- Revelation 3:14 (NIV): "These are the words of the Amen, the faithful and true witness, the ruler of God's creation."

- Revelation 4:11 (NIV): "You are worthy, our Lord and God, to receive glory and honor and power, for you created all things, and by your will they were created and have their being."

Expository Insights:

- Amen (Strong's G281): Indicates certainty and truth, emphasizing Jesus' role in creation as faithful and true.

- Ruler of God's Creation (Strong's G746): The term "ruler" (arche) signifies Jesus as the origin and source of creation.

- The doxology in Revelation 4:11 acknowledges Jesus' worthiness and sovereign power as Creator.

The Vision of the Throne Room

Key Verses: Revelation 4:2-6

In Revelation 4, John's vision of the heavenly throne room reveals the majesty and authority of Jesus as Creator, surrounded by worshippers who recognize His creative power.

- Revelation 4:2-6 (NIV): "At once I was in the Spirit, and there before me was a throne in heaven with someone sitting on it. And the one who sat there had the appearance of jasper and ruby. A rainbow that shone like an emerald encircled the throne. Surrounding the throne were twenty-four other thrones, and seated on them were twenty-four elders. They were dressed in white and had crowns of gold on their heads. From the throne came flashes of lightning, rumblings, and peals of thunder. In front of the throne, seven lamps were blazing. These are the seven spirits of God. Also in front of the throne there was what looked like a sea of glass, clear as crystal."

Expository Insights:

- Throne (Strong's G2362): Symbolizes divine sovereignty and the central authority of Jesus.

- Jasper and Ruby (Strong's G2393 and G4556): Represent God's glory and majesty.

- Rainbow (Strong's G2463): Signifies God's covenant faithfulness.

- Twenty-Four Elders (Strong's G4245): Represent the redeemed people of God, acknowledging His creative power.

- Seven Lamps and Seven Spirits (Strong's G2985 and G4151): Indicate the fullness of the Holy Spirit, involved in creation (Genesis 1:2).

The Worthy Lamb and Creation

Key Verses: Revelation 5:6-14

The depiction of Jesus as the Lamb in Revelation 5 highlights His worthiness and creative power, as all creation acknowledges His authority.

- Revelation 5:9-10 (NIV): "And they sang a new song, saying: 'You are worthy to take the scroll and to open its seals, because you were slain, and with your blood you purchased for God persons from every tribe and language and people and nation. You have made them to be a kingdom and priests to serve our God, and they will reign on the earth.'"

Expository Insights:

- Lamb (Strong's G721): Represents Jesus' sacrificial role, linking His redemptive work to His authority as Creator.

- Scroll and Seals (Strong's G975 and G4973): Symbolize the unfolding of God's plan for creation, which only Jesus can execute.

- The new song sung by the heavenly beings acknowledges Jesus' creative and redemptive work.

The Alpha and the Omega

Key Verses: Revelation 1:8, 21:6, 22:13

Jesus is proclaimed as the Alpha and the Omega, emphasizing His eternal nature and His role as the beginning and the end of all creation.

- Revelation 1:8 (NIV): "I am the Alpha and the Omega," says the Lord God, "who is, and who was, and who is to come, the Almighty."

- Revelation 21:6 (NIV): "He said to me: 'It is done. I am the Alpha and the Omega, the Beginning and the End. To the thirsty I will give water without cost from the spring of the water of life.'"

- Revelation 22:13 (NIV): "I am the Alpha and the Omega, the First and the Last, the Beginning and the End."

Expository Insights:

- Alpha and Omega (Strong's G1 and G5598): Denote Jesus as the origin and completion of all creation.

- This title underscores Jesus' sovereignty over the entire scope of creation and history.

The New Heaven and the New Earth

Key Verses: Revelation 21:1-5

The vision of the new heaven and new earth in Revelation 21 highlights Jesus' role in bringing about the ultimate renewal of creation.

- Revelation 21:1-5 (NIV): "Then I saw 'a new heaven and a new earth,' for the first heaven and the first earth had passed away, and there was no longer any sea. I saw the Holy City, the new Jerusalem, coming down out of heaven from God, prepared as a bride beautifully dressed for her husband. And I heard a loud voice from the throne saying, 'Look! God's dwelling place is now among the people, and he will dwell with them. They will be his people, and God himself will be with them and be their God. He will wipe every tear from their eyes. There will be no more death or mourning or crying or pain, for the old order of things has passed away.' He who was seated on the throne said, 'I am making everything new!' Then he said, 'Write this down, for these words are trustworthy and true.'"

Expository Insights:

- New Heaven and New Earth (Strong's G2537 and G1093): Signify the complete renewal and restoration of creation by Jesus.

- New Jerusalem (Strong's G2419): Represents the redeemed community of God's people, created anew in Christ.

- The declaration "I am making everything new" affirms Jesus' ongoing creative work in bringing about the final and perfect state of creation.

Implications for Understanding the Universe and Our Place in It

1. Jesus as the Source of All Creation: Recognizing Jesus as the Creator influences our understanding of the universe as a purposeful and divinely orchestrated reality. Everything exists by His will and through His power.

2. Humanity's Role in Creation: As part of God's creation, humans are called to steward the earth responsibly, reflecting the image of the Creator in our care for the environment and all living beings.

3. The Purpose of Creation: The ultimate purpose of creation is to glorify Jesus, the Creator. Our lives gain meaning and direction as we align ourselves with this purpose, living in a way that honors Him.

4. Hope for Renewal: The vision of the new heaven and new earth provides hope for the ultimate restoration of all things. This hope encourages believers to persevere through trials, knowing that Jesus will make all things new.

5. Intimacy with the Creator: Understanding Jesus as Creator deepens our relationship with Him. We are not merely creations but beloved children of the Creator, invited to partake in His divine life and mission.

The Book of Revelation offers a profound and majestic depiction of Jesus as the Creator. From the throne room vision to the declaration of the new heaven and new earth, Revelation affirms Jesus' preeminence and authority over all creation. As we reflect on these truths, may we be inspired to worship the Creator, steward His creation responsibly, and live with the hope of the ultimate renewal that He promises. Recognizing Jesus as the Creator transforms our understanding of the universe and our place within it, grounding us in the eternal purpose and love of God.

Jesus as Sustainer

Key Verse: Colossians 1:15-18

Lesson: Jesus is the image of the invisible God, the firstborn over all creation. By Him, all things were created in heaven and on earth, visible and invisible. He is before all things, and in Him, all things hold together.

Jesus as Sustainer: An Expository Study in the Book of Revelation

Introduction

The theme of Jesus as Sustainer is essential to Christian theology, highlighting His continuous involvement in upholding and maintaining all creation. The Book of Revelation provides profound insights into this role, depicting Jesus not only as the Creator but also as the one who holds all things together. This chapter will explore the significance of Jesus' sustaining power as exhibited in Revelation, using an expository study method with references from Strong's Concordance.

The Vision of the Risen Christ

Key Verses: Revelation 1:12-18

The opening vision of Jesus in Revelation presents Him in His glorified state, emphasizing His authority and sustaining power.

- Revelation 1:12-18 (NIV): "I turned around to see the voice that was speaking to me. And when I turned I saw seven golden lampstands, and among the lampstands was someone like a son of man, dressed in a robe reaching down to his feet and with a golden sash around his chest. The hair on his head was white like wool, as white as snow, and his eyes were like blazing fire. His feet were like bronze glowing in a furnace, and his voice was like the sound of rushing waters. In his right hand he held seven stars, and coming out of his mouth was a sharp, double-edged sword. His face was like the sun shining in all its brilliance."

Expository Insights:

- Seven Golden Lampstands (Strong's G3087): Represent the seven churches, indicating Jesus' presence and sustaining power among His people.

- Son of Man (Strong's G5207 and G444): A title that emphasizes Jesus' authority and His role as the sustainer of the church.

- Seven Stars (Strong's G792): Symbolize the angels of the seven churches, showing Jesus' control and care over the church's leadership and direction.

- Voice Like Rushing Waters (Strong's G5456): Emphasizes the power and authority of His words, sustaining creation with His command.

Jesus, the Alpha and the Omega

Key Verses: Revelation 1:8, 21:6, 22:13

Jesus is described as the Alpha and the Omega, underscoring His eternal nature and His role in sustaining all things from beginning to end.

- Revelation 1:8 (NIV): "I am the Alpha and the Omega," says the Lord God, "who is, and who was, and who is to come, the Almighty."

- Revelation 21:6 (NIV): "He said to me: 'It is done. I am the Alpha and the Omega, the Beginning and the End. To the thirsty I will give water without cost from the spring of the water of life.'"

- Revelation 22:13 (NIV): "I am the Alpha and the Omega, the First and the Last, the Beginning and the End."

Expository Insights:

- Alpha and Omega (Strong's G1 and G5598): Indicate Jesus as the origin and the conclusion of all things, emphasizing His sustaining presence throughout history.

- This title affirms Jesus' continuous role in maintaining the order and purpose of creation.

The Throne Room Vision

Key Verses: Revelation 4:2-11

John's vision of the heavenly throne room in Revelation 4 reveals the centrality of Jesus in the maintenance and sustenance of the universe.

- Revelation 4:2-6 (NIV): "At once I was in the Spirit, and there before me was a throne in heaven with someone sitting on it. And the one who sat there had the appearance of jasper and ruby. A rainbow that shone like an emerald encircled the throne. Surrounding the throne were twenty-four other thrones, and seated on them were twenty-four elders. They were dressed in white and had crowns of gold on their heads. From the throne came flashes of lightning, rumblings, and peals of thunder. In front of the throne, seven lamps were blazing. These are the seven spirits of God. Also in front of the throne there was what looked like a sea of glass, clear as crystal."

Expository Insights:

- Throne (Strong's G2362): Symbolizes divine sovereignty and Jesus' central role in sustaining creation.

- Jasper and Ruby (Strong's G2393 and G4556): Represent God's glory and sustaining presence.

- Seven Lamps and Seven Spirits (Strong's G2985 and G4151): Indicate the fullness of the Holy Spirit, actively involved in sustaining the cosmos.

The Sustaining Power of the Lamb

Key Verses: Revelation 5:6-14

The Lamb's role in Revelation 5 highlights Jesus' sustaining power through His sacrificial act and ongoing presence in creation.

- Revelation 5:6-7 (NIV): "Then I saw a Lamb, looking as if it had been slain, standing at the center of the throne, encircled by the four living creatures and the elders. The Lamb had seven horns and seven eyes, which are the seven spirits of God sent out into all the earth. He came and took the scroll from the right hand of him who sat on the throne."

Expository Insights:

- Lamb (Strong's G721): Represents Jesus' sacrificial role, highlighting the sustaining impact of His redemptive work.

- Seven Horns and Seven Eyes (Strong's G2768 and G3788): Symbolize complete power and perfect knowledge, underscoring Jesus' capacity to sustain all things through His wisdom and strength.

The New Heaven and the New Earth

Key Verses: Revelation 21:1-7

The vision of the new heaven and new earth in Revelation 21 emphasizes Jesus' role in sustaining the future state of creation, ensuring its perfection and harmony.

- Revelation 21:1-4 (NIV): "Then I saw 'a new heaven and a new earth,' for the first heaven and the first earth had passed away, and there was no longer any sea. I saw the Holy City, the new Jerusalem, coming down out of heaven from God, prepared as a bride beautifully dressed for her husband. And I heard a loud voice from the throne saying, 'Look! God's dwelling place is now among the people, and he will dwell with them. They will be his people, and God himself will be with them and be their God. He will wipe every tear from their eyes. There will be no more death or mourning or crying or pain, for the old order of things has passed away.'"

Expository Insights:

- New Heaven and New Earth (Strong's G2537 and G1093): Signify the ultimate renewal and sustainability of creation through Jesus.

- God's Dwelling with Humanity (Strong's G4637): Emphasizes the sustained presence of God with His people, ensuring their eternal well-being.

Practical Implications of Jesus as Sustainer

1. Trust in His Provision: Understanding Jesus as Sustainer encourages believers to trust in His provision and care in all circumstances. He upholds the universe and ensures our needs are met.

2. Strength in Trials: Jesus' sustaining power provides strength and endurance during trials and challenges. Knowing He holds all things together gives us the confidence to face difficulties with hope.

3. Stewardship of Creation: Recognizing Jesus' role in sustaining creation inspires us to be responsible stewards of the environment and all that God has entrusted to us.

4. Unity in the Church: Jesus sustains the church, and His presence among the lampstands signifies His ongoing involvement and guidance. This fosters unity and cooperation within the body of Christ.

5. Hope for the Future: The vision of the new heaven and new earth assures us of the future renewal and perfection of all things. This hope sustains us as we navigate the brokenness of the present world.

The Book of Revelation provides a majestic and powerful depiction of Jesus as Sustainer. From the vision of the risen Christ to the proclamation of the Alpha and Omega, and from the throne room scenes to the promise of a new creation, Revelation affirms Jesus' continuous role in upholding and maintaining all things. As we reflect on these truths, we are encouraged to trust in His provision, find strength in His sustaining power, and live as responsible stewards of His creation. Recognizing Jesus as Sustainer transforms our understanding of the universe and our daily lives, grounding us in the eternal care and purpose of God.

The Eternal Sovereignty of Jesus as Exhibited in the Book of Revelation

Introduction

The Book of Revelation, the final book of the Bible, presents a vivid and awe-inspiring picture of Jesus Christ's eternal sovereignty. Written by the Apostle John during his exile on the island of Patmos, Revelation is a prophetic vision that reveals the ultimate triumph of Christ over evil and His eternal reign. This chapter will explore the eternal sovereignty of Jesus as depicted in Revelation, using an expository study method and exhaustive references from Strong's Concordance to unpack the rich symbolism and powerful declarations of Christ's supremacy.

The Alpha and the Omega

Key Verses: Revelation 1:8, 22:13

Jesus is introduced as the Alpha and the Omega, the beginning and the end. This title, derived from the first and last letters of the Greek alphabet, signifies Jesus' eternal existence and His sovereign authority over all of history.

- Revelation 1:8 (NIV): "I am the Alpha and the Omega," says the Lord God, "who is, and who was, and who is to come, the Almighty."

- Revelation 22:13 (NIV): "I am the Alpha and the Omega, the First and the Last, the Beginning and the End."

Expository Insights:

- The term Alpha (Strong's G1) and Omega (Strong's G5598) emphasize Jesus' eternal nature and His role as the Creator and Consummator of all things.

- This title affirms that Jesus is sovereign over time and existence, encompassing the entirety of creation and its ultimate destiny.

The Vision of the Risen Christ

Key Verses: Revelation 1:12-18

John's vision of the risen Christ in Revelation 1 provides a powerful depiction of Jesus' majesty and authority. This passage describes Jesus in His glorified state, revealing His divine attributes and eternal sovereignty.

- Revelation 1:12-16 (NIV): John describes seeing Jesus standing among seven golden lampstands, with a robe reaching down to His feet and a golden sash around His chest. His head and hair were white like wool, as white as snow, and His eyes were like blazing fire. His feet were like bronze glowing in a furnace, and His voice was like the sound of rushing waters. In His right hand, He held seven stars, and out of His mouth came a sharp double-edged sword. His face was like the sun shining in all its brilliance.

Expository Insights:

- Seven Golden Lampstands (Strong's G3087): Represent the seven churches, indicating Jesus' presence and authority among His people.

- White Hair (Strong's G3022): Symbolizes purity and eternal wisdom.

- Blazing Eyes (Strong's G3788): Denote His penetrating vision and omniscience.

- Glowing Feet (Strong's G5474): Represent judgment and strength.

- Voice Like Rushing Waters (Strong's G5456): Emphasizes the power and authority of His words.

- Double-edged Sword (Strong's G4501): Symbolizes the penetrating power of His truth and judgment.

- Face Like the Sun (Strong's G2246): Reflects His divine glory and brilliance.

The Lamb Who Was Slain

Key Verses: Revelation 5:6-14

In Revelation 5, Jesus is depicted as the Lamb who was slain, a powerful symbol of His sacrificial death and victorious resurrection. This passage highlights His worthiness to open the scroll and execute God's redemptive plan.

- Revelation 5:6-7 (NIV): "Then I saw a Lamb, looking as if it had been slain, standing in the center of the throne, encircled by the four living creatures and the elders. He had seven horns and seven eyes, which are the seven spirits of God sent out into all the earth. He came and took the scroll from the right hand of him who sat on the throne."

Expository Insights:

- Lamb (Strong's G721): Represents Jesus as the sacrificial Lamb of God who takes away the sins of the world (John 1:29).

- Seven Horns (Strong's G2768): Symbolize complete power and authority.

- Seven Eyes (Strong's G3788): Represent perfect knowledge and the omnipresence of the Holy Spirit.

- The act of taking the scroll signifies Jesus' unique authority to carry out God's sovereign will and judgment.

King of Kings and Lord of Lords

Key Verses: Revelation 19:11-16

Revelation 19 presents Jesus as the triumphant King of Kings and Lord of Lords, leading the heavenly armies to victory over the forces of evil. This powerful image underscores His ultimate authority and eternal reign.

- Revelation 19:11-16 (NIV): "I saw heaven standing open and there before me was a white horse, whose rider is called Faithful and True. With justice he judges and makes war. His eyes are like blazing fire, and on his head are many crowns. He has a name written on him that no one knows but he himself. He is dressed in a robe dipped in blood, and his name is the Word of God. The armies of heaven were following him, riding on white horses and dressed in fine linen, white and clean. Out of his mouth comes a sharp sword with which to strike down the nations. He will rule them with an iron scepter. He treads the winepress of the fury of the wrath of God Almighty. On his robe and on his thigh he has this name written: KING OF KINGS AND LORD OF LORDS."

Expository Insights:

- White Horse (Strong's G3022): Symbolizes victory and purity.

- Faithful and True (Strong's G4103 and G228): Titles that emphasize Jesus' reliability and integrity.

- Many Crowns (Strong's G1238): Represent His supreme authority over all earthly and heavenly realms.

- Word of God (Strong's G3056): Highlights Jesus' role as the divine Logos, the ultimate revelation of God.

- Iron Scepter (Strong's G4464): Symbolizes His unyielding rule and judgment.

The New Heaven and the New Earth

Key Verses: Revelation 21:1-7

The final chapters of Revelation describe the establishment of a new heaven and a new earth, where Jesus reigns eternally with His people. This ultimate renewal of creation underscores Jesus' sovereignty and His role in bringing about the fulfillment of God's redemptive plan.

- Revelation 21:1-4 (NIV): "Then I saw a new heaven and a new earth, for the first heaven and the first earth had passed away, and there was no longer any sea. I saw the Holy City, the new Jerusalem, coming down out of heaven from God, prepared as a bride beautifully dressed for her husband. And I heard a loud voice from the throne saying, 'Now the dwelling of God is with men, and he will live with them. They will be his people, and God himself will be with them and be their God. He will wipe every tear from their eyes. There will be no more death or mourning or crying or pain, for the old order of things has passed away.'"

Expository Insights:

- New Heaven and New Earth (Strong's G2537 and G1093): Symbolize the complete renewal and restoration of creation.

- New Jerusalem (Strong's G2419): Represents the redeemed community of God's people.

- God's Dwelling with Humanity (Strong's G4637): Emphasizes the intimate and eternal relationship between God and His people.

- The elimination of death, mourning, crying, and pain signifies the ultimate victory of Jesus over all forms of evil and suffering.

The Book of Revelation provides a majestic and awe-inspiring depiction of Jesus Christ's eternal sovereignty. From the vision of the risen Christ to His portrayal as the Lamb who was slain, and from His triumphant return as King of Kings to the establishment of a new heaven and new earth, Revelation affirms the supreme authority and eternal reign of Jesus. These vivid images and powerful declarations offer hope and assurance to believers, reminding us of the ultimate victory of Christ and the fulfillment of God's redemptive plan. As we reflect on these truths, may we be encouraged to live faithfully under the lordship of Jesus, our eternal sovereign.

CHAPTER 02

THE FULLNESS OF DEITY IN CHRIST

Key Verse: Colossians 2:9-10

Lesson: In Christ, all the fullness of the Deity lives in bodily form, and in Him, you have been brought to fullness. He is the head over every power and authority.

The Fullness of Deity in Christ: An Expository Study in the Book of Revelation

Introduction

The fullness of deity in Christ is a central theme in Christian theology, emphasizing that Jesus embodies the complete nature and essence of God. This truth is powerfully illustrated in the Book of Revelation, which presents vivid and majestic images of Jesus' divine nature and authority. This chapter will explore the lesson of the fullness of deity in Christ as exhibited in Revelation, using an expository study method with references from Strong's Concordance to deepen our understanding.

Jesus as the Alpha and the Omega

Key Verses: Revelation 1:8, 21:6, 22:13

Revelation explicitly proclaims Jesus as the Alpha and the Omega, highlighting His eternal and divine nature.

- Revelation 1:8 (NIV): "I am the Alpha and the Omega," says the Lord God, "who is, and who was, and who is to come, the Almighty."

- Revelation 21:6 (NIV): "He said to me: 'It is done. I am the Alpha and the Omega, the Beginning and the End. To the thirsty I will give water without cost from the spring of the water of life.'"

- Revelation 22:13 (NIV): "I am the Alpha and the Omega, the First and the Last, the Beginning and the End."

Expository Insights:

- Alpha and Omega (Strong's G1 and G5598): Represent the first and last letters of the Greek alphabet, indicating Jesus' eternal existence and His encompassing presence in all things.

- The Almighty (Strong's G3841): Affirms Jesus' supreme power and authority over all creation, reflecting His divine nature.

The Vision of the Glorified Christ

Key Verses: Revelation 1:12-18

John's vision of the glorified Christ in Revelation 1 reveals the fullness of Jesus' deity through powerful imagery and descriptions.

- Revelation 1:12-18 (NIV): "I turned around to see the voice that was speaking to me. And when I turned I saw seven golden lampstands, and among the lampstands was someone like a son of man, dressed in a robe reaching down to his feet and with a golden sash around his chest. The hair on his head was white like wool, as white as snow, and his eyes were like blazing fire. His feet were like bronze glowing in a furnace, and his voice was like the sound of rushing waters. In his right hand he held seven stars, and coming out of his mouth was a sharp, double-edged sword. His face was like the sun shining in all its brilliance."

Expository Insights:

- Seven Golden Lampstands (Strong's G3087): Represent the seven churches, indicating Jesus' presence among His people.

- Son of Man (Strong's G5207 and G444): A messianic title that emphasizes Jesus' humanity and divinity, rooted in Daniel 7:13-14.

- White Hair (Strong's G3022): Symbolizes purity, holiness, and eternal wisdom, reflecting the Ancient of Days (Daniel 7:9).

- Blazing Eyes (Strong's G3788): Denote His penetrating vision and omniscience.

- Glowing Feet (Strong's G5474): Represent judgment and strength.

- Voice Like Rushing Waters (Strong's G5456): Emphasizes the power and authority of His words.

- Double-edged Sword (Strong's G4501): Symbolizes the discerning and powerful nature of His word.

- Face Like the Sun (Strong's G2246): Reflects His divine glory and brilliance.

The Worthy Lamb

Key Verses: Revelation 5:6-14

The depiction of Jesus as the Lamb in Revelation 5 underscores His worthiness and divine authority, encompassing the fullness of God's nature.

- Revelation 5:6-7 (NIV): "Then I saw a Lamb, looking as if it had been slain, standing at the center of the throne, encircled by the four living creatures and the elders. The

Lamb had seven horns and seven eyes, which are the seven spirits of God sent out into all the earth. He came and took the scroll from the right hand of him who sat on the throne."

Expository Insights:

- Lamb (Strong's G721): Represents Jesus' sacrificial role, highlighting His redemptive work.

- Seven Horns and Seven Eyes (Strong's G2768 and G3788): Symbolize complete power and perfect knowledge, underscoring Jesus' omnipotence and omniscience.

- Seven Spirits of God (Strong's G4151): Indicate the fullness of the Holy Spirit, reflecting the divine nature of Jesus.

Jesus as the Divine Judge

Key Verses: Revelation 19:11-16

Revelation 19 presents Jesus as the divine judge, emphasizing His authority and the fullness of His deity in executing righteous judgment.

- Revelation 19:11-16 (NIV): "I saw heaven standing open and there before me was a white horse, whose rider is called Faithful and True. With justice he judges and wages war. His eyes are like blazing fire, and on his head are many crowns. He has a name written on him that no one knows but he himself. He is dressed in a robe dipped in blood, and his name is the Word of God. The armies of heaven were following him, riding on white horses and dressed in fine linen, white and clean. Coming out of his mouth is a sharp sword with which to strike down the nations. 'He will rule them with an iron scepter.' He treads the winepress of the fury of the wrath of God Almighty. On his robe and on his thigh he has this name written: KING OF KINGS AND LORD OF LORDS."

Expository Insights:

- White Horse (Strong's G3022): Symbolizes victory and purity.

- Faithful and True (Strong's G4103 and G228): Titles that emphasize Jesus' reliability and integrity.

- Many Crowns (Strong's G1238): Represent His supreme authority over all earthly and heavenly realms.

- Word of God (Strong's G3056): Highlights Jesus' role as the divine Logos, the ultimate revelation of God (John 1:1).

- Iron Scepter (Strong's G4464): Symbolizes His unyielding rule and judgment.

The New Heaven and the New Earth

Key Verses: Revelation 21:1-7

The vision of the new heaven and new earth in Revelation 21 underscores the fullness of Jesus' deity in bringing about the ultimate renewal of creation.

- Revelation 21:1-4 (NIV): "Then I saw 'a new heaven and a new earth,' for the first heaven and the first earth had passed away, and there was no longer any sea. I saw the Holy City, the new Jerusalem, coming down out of heaven from God, prepared as a bride beautifully dressed for her husband. And I heard a loud voice from the throne saying, 'Look! God's dwelling place is now among the people, and he will dwell with them. They will be his people, and God himself will be with them and be their God. He will wipe every tear from their eyes. There will be no more death or mourning or crying or pain, for the old order of things has passed away.'"

Expository Insights:

- New Heaven and New Earth (Strong's G2537 and G1093): Signify the complete renewal and restoration of creation by Jesus.

- New Jerusalem (Strong's G2419): Represents the redeemed community of God's people, created anew in Christ.

- God's Dwelling with Humanity (Strong's G4637): Emphasizes the intimate and eternal relationship between God and His people.

- The elimination of death, mourning, crying, and pain signifies the ultimate victory of Jesus over all forms of evil and suffering.

Practical Implications of the Fullness of Deity in Christ

1. Complete in Christ: Recognizing the fullness of deity in Christ assures us that in Him, we have all we need for spiritual growth and maturity. We are made complete in Him.

2. Authority and Power: Jesus' divine nature means He has ultimate authority over all powers and authorities. This gives us confidence and security in His sovereign rule.

3. Intimate Relationship: Understanding Jesus as fully God deepens our relationship with Him. We are not just followers of a great teacher but are united with the living God.

4. Eternal Hope: The fullness of deity in Christ assures us of our eternal hope and future. We can look forward to the new heaven and new earth where we will dwell with God forever.

5. Empowered Living: Knowing that Jesus embodies all the fullness of God empowers us to live boldly and faithfully, reflecting His character in our lives.

Conclusion

The Book of Revelation vividly portrays the fullness of deity in Christ through powerful imagery and declarations. From Jesus' proclamation as the Alpha and Omega to the vision of the glorified Christ, and from the worthy Lamb to the divine judge, Revelation affirms the complete nature and authority of

Jesus. As we reflect on these truths, we are encouraged to embrace our completeness in Him, live under His authority, and anticipate the eternal hope we have in Him. Recognizing the fullness of deity in Christ transforms our understanding of His divine nature and our relationship with Him, grounding us in the eternal purpose and love of God.

Fullness of Deity

Key Verse: Colossians 2:9-10

Lesson: In Christ, all the fullness of the Deity lives in bodily form, and in Him, you have been brought to fullness. He is the head over every power and authority.

Fullness of Deity: An Expository Study in the Book of Revelation

Introduction

The mystery of the incarnation—God becoming fully human in Jesus Christ—is a cornerstone of Christian faith. This profound truth asserts that in Jesus, the fullness of the deity dwells bodily, making Him both fully God and fully man. The Book of Revelation presents a vivid and majestic depiction of Jesus' divine nature, emphasizing His supreme authority and eternal sovereignty. This chapter will explore the fullness of deity in Christ as exhibited in Revelation, using an expository study method with references from Strong's Concordance.

The Alpha and the Omega

Key Verses: Revelation 1:8, 21:6, 22:13

Jesus is introduced as the Alpha and the Omega, a title that underscores His eternal and divine nature, and thus, His fullness as God.

- Revelation 1:8 (NIV): "I am the Alpha and the Omega," says the Lord God, "who is, and who was, and who is to come, the Almighty."

- Revelation 21:6 (NIV): "He said to me: 'It is done. I am the Alpha and the Omega, the Beginning and the End. To the thirsty I will give water without cost from the spring of the water of life.'"

- Revelation 22:13 (NIV): "I am the Alpha and the Omega, the First and the Last, the Beginning and the End."

Expository Insights:

- Alpha and Omega (Strong's G1 and G5598): Represent the first and last letters of the Greek alphabet, indicating Jesus' eternal existence and His encompassing presence in all things.

- The Almighty (Strong's G3841): Affirms Jesus' supreme power and authority over all creation, reflecting His divine nature.

The Vision of the Glorified Christ

Key Verses: Revelation 1:12-18

John's vision of the glorified Christ provides a powerful representation of Jesus' divine attributes and the fullness of His deity.

- Revelation 1:12-18 (NIV): "I turned around to see the voice that was speaking to me. And when I turned I saw seven golden lampstands, and among the lampstands was someone like a son of man, dressed in a robe reaching down to his feet and with a golden sash around his chest. The hair on his head was white like wool, as white as snow, and his eyes were like blazing fire. His feet were like bronze glowing in a furnace, and his voice was like the sound of rushing waters. In his right hand he held seven stars, and coming out of his mouth was a sharp, double-edged sword. His face was like the sun shining in all its brilliance."

Expository Insights:

- Seven Golden Lampstands (Strong's G3087): Represent the seven churches, indicating Jesus' presence among His people.

- Son of Man (Strong's G5207 and G444): A messianic title that emphasizes Jesus' humanity and divinity, rooted in Daniel 7:13-14.

- White Hair (Strong's G3022): Symbolizes purity, holiness, and eternal wisdom, reflecting the Ancient of Days (Daniel 7:9).

- Blazing Eyes (Strong's G3788): Denote His penetrating vision and omniscience.

- Glowing Feet (Strong's G5474): Represent judgment and strength.

- Voice Like Rushing Waters (Strong's G5456): Emphasizes the power and authority of His words.

- Double-edged Sword (Strong's G4501): Symbolizes the discerning and powerful nature of His word.

- Face Like the Sun (Strong's G2246): Reflects His divine glory and brilliance.

The Lamb Who Was Slain

Key Verses: Revelation 5:6-14

Revelation 5 presents Jesus as the Lamb who was slain, a powerful image that combines His sacrificial role with His divine authority.

- Revelation 5:6-7 (NIV): "Then I saw a Lamb, looking as if it had been slain, standing at the center of the throne, encircled by the four living creatures and the elders. The Lamb had seven horns and seven eyes, which are the seven spirits of God sent out into all the earth. He came and took the scroll from the right hand of him who sat on the throne."

Expository Insights:

- Lamb (Strong's G721): Represents Jesus' sacrificial role, highlighting His redemptive work.

- Seven Horns and Seven Eyes (Strong's G2768 and G3788): Symbolize complete power and perfect knowledge, underscoring Jesus' omnipotence and omniscience.

- Seven Spirits of God (Strong's G4151): Indicate the fullness of the Holy Spirit, reflecting the divine nature of Jesus.

Jesus as the Divine Judge

Key Verses: Revelation 19:11-16

In Revelation 19, Jesus is depicted as the divine judge, emphasizing His authority and the fullness of His deity in executing righteous judgment.

- Revelation 19:11-16 (NIV): "I saw heaven standing open and there before me was a white horse, whose rider is called Faithful and True. With justice he judges and wages war. His eyes are like blazing fire, and on his head are many crowns. He has a name written on him that no one knows but he himself. He is dressed in a robe dipped in blood, and his name is the Word of God. The armies of heaven were following him, riding on white horses and dressed in fine linen, white and clean. Coming out of his mouth is a sharp sword with which to strike down the nations. 'He will rule them with an iron scepter.' He treads the winepress of the fury of the wrath of God Almighty. On his robe and on his thigh he has this name written: KING OF KINGS AND LORD OF LORDS."

Expository Insights:

- White Horse (Strong's G3022): Symbolizes victory and purity.

- Faithful and True (Strong's G4103 and G228): Titles that emphasize Jesus' reliability and integrity.

- Many Crowns (Strong's G1238): Represent His supreme authority over all earthly and heavenly realms.

- Word of God (Strong's G3056): Highlights Jesus' role as the divine Logos, the ultimate revelation of God (John 1:1).

- Iron Scepter (Strong's G4464): Symbolizes His unyielding rule and judgment.

The New Heaven and the New Earth

Key Verses: Revelation 21:1-7

The vision of the new heaven and new earth in Revelation 21 emphasizes Jesus' role in bringing about the ultimate renewal of creation, showcasing the fullness of His deity.

- Revelation 21:1-4 (NIV): "Then I saw 'a new heaven and a new earth,' for the first heaven and the first earth had passed away, and there was no longer any sea. I saw the Holy City, the new Jerusalem, coming down out of heaven from God, prepared as a bride beautifully dressed for her husband. And I heard a loud voice from the throne saying, 'Look! God's dwelling place is now among the people, and he will dwell with them. They will be his people, and God himself will be with them and be their God. He will wipe every tear from their eyes. There will be no more death or mourning or crying or pain, for the old order of things has passed away.'"

Expository Insights:

- New Heaven and New Earth (Strong's G2537 and G1093): Signify the complete renewal and restoration of creation by Jesus.

- New Jerusalem (Strong's G2419): Represents the redeemed community of God's people, created anew in Christ.

- God's Dwelling with Humanity (Strong's G4637): Emphasizes the intimate and eternal relationship between God and His people.

- The elimination of death, mourning, crying, and pain signifies the ultimate victory of Jesus over all forms of evil and suffering.

Practical Implications of the Fullness of Deity in Christ

1. Complete in Christ: Recognizing the fullness of deity in Christ assures us that in Him, we have all we need for spiritual growth and maturity. We are made complete in Him.

2. Authority and Power: Jesus' divine nature means He has ultimate authority over all powers and authorities. This gives us confidence and security in His sovereign rule.

3. Intimate Relationship: Understanding Jesus as fully God deepens our relationship with Him. We are not just followers of a great teacher but are united with the living God.

4. Eternal Hope: The fullness of deity in Christ assures us of our eternal hope and future. We can look forward to the new heaven and new earth where we will dwell with God forever.

5. Empowered Living: Knowing that Jesus embodies all the fullness of God empowers us to live boldly and faithfully, reflecting His character in our lives.

Conclusion

The Book of Revelation vividly portrays the fullness of deity in Christ through powerful imagery and declarations. From Jesus' proclamation as the Alpha and Omega to the vision of the glorified Christ, and from the worthy Lamb to the divine judge, Revelation affirms the complete nature and authority of Jesus. As we reflect on these truths, we are encouraged to embrace our completeness in Him, live under His authority, and anticipate the eternal hope we have in Him. Recognizing the fullness of deity in Christ transforms our understanding of His divine nature and our relationship with Him, grounding us in the eternal purpose and love of God.

Complete in Christ

Key Verse: Colossians 2:9-10

Lesson: In Christ, all the fullness of the Deity lives in bodily form, and in Him, you have been brought to fullness. He is the head over every power and authority.

Complete in Christ: An Expository Study in the Book of Revelation

Introduction

The concept of being "complete in Christ" is a profound truth in Christian theology. It signifies that believers, through their union with Jesus, lack nothing for their spiritual journey and salvation. This completeness encompasses spiritual maturity, authority, and sufficiency, all derived from the fullness of Christ's deity. The Book of Revelation, with its vivid and powerful imagery, provides deep insights into how believers are made complete in Christ. This chapter will explore this theme, using an expository study method with references from Strong's Concordance.

Jesus, the Alpha and the Omega

Key Verses: Revelation 1:8, 21:6, 22:13

Revelation highlights Jesus as the Alpha and the Omega, emphasizing His eternal nature and His role in completing our faith.

- Revelation 1:8 (NIV): "I am the Alpha and the Omega," says the Lord God, "who is, and who was, and who is to come, the Almighty."

- Revelation 21:6 (NIV): "He said to me: 'It is done. I am the Alpha and the Omega, the Beginning and the End. To the thirsty I will give water without cost from the spring of the water of life.'"

- Revelation 22:13 (NIV): "I am the Alpha and the Omega, the First and the Last, the Beginning and the End."

Expository Insights:

- Alpha and Omega (Strong's G1 and G5598): Indicate Jesus' eternal existence and His role in the beginning and completion of all things.

- This title assures believers that their faith journey is encompassed within Christ's eternal framework, ensuring they lack nothing.

The Vision of the Glorified Christ

Key Verses: Revelation 1:12-18

John's vision of the glorified Christ presents a powerful image of Jesus' divine authority and sufficiency, which is the foundation for believers' completeness in Him.

- Revelation 1:12-18 (NIV): "I turned around to see the voice that was speaking to me. And when I turned I saw seven golden lampstands, and among the lampstands was someone like a son of man, dressed in a robe reaching down to his feet and with a golden sash around his chest. The hair on his head was white like wool, as white as snow, and his eyes were like blazing fire. His feet were like bronze glowing in a furnace, and his voice was like the sound of rushing waters. In his right hand he held seven stars, and coming out of his mouth was a sharp, double-edged sword. His face was like the sun shining in all its brilliance."

Expository Insights:

- Seven Golden Lampstands (Strong's G3087): Represent the seven churches, indicating Jesus' presence and sustaining power among His people.

- Son of Man (Strong's G5207 and G444): A title emphasizing Jesus' humanity and divinity.

- Seven Stars (Strong's G792): Symbolize the angels of the seven churches, showing Jesus' control and care over the church's leadership and direction.

- Voice Like Rushing Waters (Strong's G5456): Emphasizes the power and authority of His words, which sustain and guide believers.

- This vision assures believers that in Christ, they are under divine authority and care, ensuring their completeness.

The Worthy Lamb

Key Verses: Revelation 5:6-14

Revelation 5 depicts Jesus as the Lamb who was slain, a powerful symbol of His redemptive work and divine authority, ensuring believers' completeness in Him.

- Revelation 5:6-7 (NIV): "Then I saw a Lamb, looking as if it had been slain, standing at the center of the throne, encircled by the four living creatures and the elders. The Lamb had seven horns and seven eyes, which are the seven spirits of God sent out into all the earth. He came and took the scroll from the right hand of him who sat on the throne."

Expository Insights:

- Lamb (Strong's G721): Represents Jesus' sacrificial role, highlighting His redemptive work.

- Seven Horns and Seven Eyes (Strong's G2768 and G3788): Symbolize complete power and perfect knowledge, underscoring Jesus' omnipotence and omniscience.

- Seven Spirits of God (Strong's G4151): Indicate the fullness of the Holy Spirit, reflecting the divine nature of Jesus.

- The Lamb's worthiness assures believers that in Christ, they have access to the fullness of God's redemptive power and knowledge, ensuring their spiritual completeness.

Jesus as the Divine Judge

Key Verses: Revelation 19:11-16

Revelation 19 portrays Jesus as the divine judge, highlighting His authority and the fullness of His deity, ensuring believers' victory and completeness in Him.

- Revelation 19:11-16 (NIV): "I saw heaven standing open and there before me was a white horse, whose rider is called Faithful and True. With justice he judges and wages war. His eyes are like blazing fire, and on his head are many crowns. He has a name written on him that no one knows but he himself. He is dressed in a robe dipped in blood, and his name is the Word of God. The armies of heaven were following him, riding on white horses and dressed in fine linen, white and clean. Coming out of his mouth is a sharp sword with which to strike down the nations. 'He will rule them with an iron scepter.' He treads the winepress of the fury of the wrath of God Almighty. On his robe and on his thigh he has this name written: KING OF KINGS AND LORD OF LORDS."

Expository Insights:

- White Horse (Strong's G3022): Symbolizes victory and purity.

- Faithful and True (Strong's G4103 and G228): Titles that emphasize Jesus' reliability and integrity.

- Many Crowns (Strong's G1238): Represent His supreme authority over all earthly and heavenly realms.

- Word of God (Strong's G3056): Highlights Jesus' role as the divine Logos, the ultimate revelation of God (John 1:1).

- Iron Scepter (Strong's G4464): Symbolizes His unyielding rule and judgment.

- This portrayal assures believers that in Christ, they are victorious and complete, under His supreme authority.

The New Heaven and the New Earth

Key Verses: Revelation 21:1-7

The vision of the new heaven and new earth in Revelation 21 emphasizes the ultimate completion and fulfillment found in Christ.

- Revelation 21:1-4 (NIV): "Then I saw 'a new heaven and a new earth,' for the first heaven and the first earth had passed away, and there was no longer any sea. I saw the Holy

City, the new Jerusalem, coming down out of heaven from God, prepared as a bride beautifully dressed for her husband. And I heard a loud voice from the throne saying, 'Look! God's dwelling place is now among the people, and he will dwell with them. They will be his people, and God himself will be with them and be their God. He will wipe every tear from their eyes. There will be no more death or mourning or crying or pain, for the old order of things has passed away.'"

Expository Insights:

- New Heaven and New Earth (Strong's G2537 and G1093): Signify the complete renewal and restoration of creation by Jesus.

- New Jerusalem (Strong's G2419): Represents the redeemed community of God's people, created anew in Christ.

- God's Dwelling with Humanity (Strong's G4637): Emphasizes the intimate and eternal relationship between God and His people.

- The elimination of death, mourning, crying, and pain signifies the ultimate victory and completeness found in Jesus.

Practical Implications of Being Complete in Christ

1. Spiritual Maturity: Recognizing our completeness in Christ encourages believers to pursue spiritual maturity, knowing they lack nothing for their growth.

2. Authority and Security: Believers can live confidently, knowing they are under the supreme authority and care of Jesus.

3. Intimate Relationship: Understanding our completeness in Christ deepens our relationship with Him, fostering a closer walk with God.

4. Hope and Assurance: The promise of the new heaven and new earth provides hope and assurance, motivating believers to persevere through trials.

5. Empowered Living: Knowing that we are complete in Christ empowers us to live boldly and faithfully, reflecting His character in our lives.

Conclusion

The Book of Revelation vividly portrays the completeness believers have in Christ through powerful imagery and declarations. From Jesus' proclamation as the Alpha and Omega to the vision of the glorified Christ, and from the worthy Lamb to the divine judge, Revelation affirms the sufficiency and authority of Jesus. As we reflect on these truths, we are encouraged to embrace our completeness in Him, live under His authority, and anticipate the eternal hope we have in Him. Recognizing our completeness in Christ transforms our understanding of our spiritual journey and our relationship with Him, grounding us in the eternal purpose and love of God.

Authority of Christ

Key Verse: Colossians 2:9-10

Lesson: In Christ, all the fullness of the Deity lives in bodily form, and in Him, you have been brought to fullness. He is the head over every power and authority.

Authority of Christ: An Expository Study in the Book of Revelation

Introduction

The authority of Jesus Christ is a central theme in Christian theology, underscoring His supremacy over all spiritual and earthly powers. The Book of Revelation, with its vivid imagery and powerful declarations, presents a comprehensive picture of Christ's ultimate authority. This chapter will explore the significance of Jesus' authority as exhibited in Revelation, using an expository study method with references from Strong's Concordance.

Jesus as the Alpha and the Omega

Key Verses: Revelation 1:8, 21:6, 22:13

Revelation introduces Jesus as the Alpha and the Omega, emphasizing His eternal nature and supreme authority.

- Revelation 1:8 (NIV): "I am the Alpha and the Omega," says the Lord God, "who is, and who was, and who is to come, the Almighty."

- Revelation 21:6 (NIV): "He said to me: 'It is done. I am the Alpha and the Omega, the Beginning and the End. To the thirsty I will give water without cost from the spring of the water of life.'"

- Revelation 22:13 (NIV): "I am the Alpha and the Omega, the First and the Last, the Beginning and the End."

Expository Insights:

- Alpha and Omega (Strong's G1 and G5598): Indicate Jesus' eternal existence and His encompassing authority over all time and creation.

- The Almighty (Strong's G3841): Affirms Jesus' supreme power and authority over all creation, reflecting His divine nature.

The Vision of the Glorified Christ

Key Verses: Revelation 1:12-18

John's vision of the glorified Christ presents a powerful image of Jesus' divine authority and majesty.

- Revelation 1:12-18 (NIV): "I turned around to see the voice that was speaking to me. And when I turned I saw seven golden lampstands, and among the lampstands was someone like a son of man, dressed in a robe reaching down to his feet and with a golden sash around his chest. The hair on his head was white like wool, as white as snow, and his eyes were like blazing fire. His feet were like bronze glowing in a furnace, and his voice was like the sound of rushing waters. In his right hand he held seven stars, and coming out of his mouth was a sharp, double-edged sword. His face was like the sun shining in all its brilliance."

Expository Insights:

- Seven Golden Lampstands (Strong's G3087): Represent the seven churches, indicating Jesus' presence and authority among His people.

- Son of Man (Strong's G5207 and G444): A title emphasizing Jesus' humanity and divinity, rooted in Daniel 7:13-14.

- Seven Stars (Strong's G792): Symbolize the angels of the seven churches, showing Jesus' control and care over the church's leadership and direction.

- Voice Like Rushing Waters (Strong's G5456): Emphasizes the power and authority of His words.

- This vision underscores Jesus' authority over the church and His role as the sovereign ruler.

The Worthy Lamb

Key Verses: Revelation 5:6-14

Revelation 5 depicts Jesus as the Lamb who was slain, highlighting His worthiness and authority to execute God's redemptive plan.

- Revelation 5:6-7 (NIV): "Then I saw a Lamb, looking as if it had been slain, standing at the center of the throne, encircled by the four living creatures and the elders. The Lamb had seven horns and seven eyes, which are the seven spirits of God sent out into all the earth. He came and took the scroll from the right hand of him who sat on the throne."

Expository Insights:

- Lamb (Strong's G721): Represents Jesus' sacrificial role, highlighting His redemptive work.

- Seven Horns and Seven Eyes (Strong's G2768 and G3788): Symbolize complete power and perfect knowledge, underscoring Jesus' omnipotence and omniscience.

- Seven Spirits of God (Strong's G4151): Indicate the fullness of the Holy Spirit, reflecting the divine nature of Jesus.

- The Lamb's worthiness to open the scroll signifies His authority to execute God's plan for redemption and judgment.

Jesus as the Divine Judge

Key Verses: Revelation 19:11-16

In Revelation 19, Jesus is portrayed as the divine judge, emphasizing His authority over all nations and His role in executing final judgment.

- Revelation 19:11-16 (NIV): "I saw heaven standing open and there before me was a white horse, whose rider is called Faithful and True. With justice he judges and wages war. His eyes are like blazing fire, and on his head are many crowns. He has a name written on him that no one knows but he himself. He is dressed in a robe dipped in blood, and his name is the Word of God. The armies of heaven were following him, riding on white horses and dressed in fine linen, white and clean. Coming out of his mouth is a sharp sword with which to strike down the nations. 'He will rule them with an iron scepter.' He treads the winepress of the fury of the wrath of God Almighty. On his robe and on his thigh he has this name written: KING OF KINGS AND LORD OF LORDS."

Expository Insights:

- White Horse (Strong's G3022): Symbolizes victory and purity.

- Faithful and True (Strong's G4103 and G228): Titles that emphasize Jesus' reliability and integrity.

- Many Crowns (Strong's G1238): Represent His supreme authority over all earthly and heavenly realms.

- Word of God (Strong's G3056): Highlights Jesus' role as the divine Logos, the ultimate revelation of God (John 1:1).

- Iron Scepter (Strong's G4464): Symbolizes His unyielding rule and judgment.

- This portrayal emphasizes Jesus' ultimate authority and His role in executing divine justice.

The New Heaven and the New Earth

Key Verses: Revelation 21:1-7

The vision of the new heaven and new earth in Revelation 21 underscores Jesus' authority in bringing about the ultimate renewal of creation.

- Revelation 21:1-4 (NIV): "Then I saw 'a new heaven and a new earth,' for the first heaven and the first earth had passed away, and there was no longer any sea. I saw the Holy City, the new Jerusalem, coming down out of heaven from God, prepared as a bride beautifully dressed for her husband. And I heard a loud voice from the throne saying, 'Look! God's dwelling place is now among the people, and he will dwell with them. They will be his people, and God himself will be with them and be their God. He will wipe every tear from their eyes. There will be no more death or mourning or crying or pain, for the old order of things has passed away.'"

Expository Insights:

- New Heaven and New Earth (Strong's G2537 and G1093): Signify the complete renewal and restoration of creation by Jesus.

- New Jerusalem (Strong's G2419): Represents the redeemed community of God's people, created anew in Christ.

- God's Dwelling with Humanity (Strong's G4637): Emphasizes the intimate and eternal relationship between God and His people.

- The elimination of death, mourning, crying, and pain signifies the ultimate victory and authority of Jesus over all forms of evil and suffering.

Practical Implications of Jesus' Authority

1. Confidence in His Sovereignty: Recognizing Jesus' authority over all spiritual and earthly powers provides believers with confidence in His sovereignty and control over every aspect of life.

2. Submission to His Rule: Understanding Jesus' authority calls believers to submit to His rule and align their lives with His will.

3. Assurance of Victory: Jesus' authority assures believers of ultimate victory over sin, death, and evil, encouraging perseverance in faith.

4. Empowerment for Mission: Jesus' authority empowers believers to engage in His mission with boldness, knowing they operate under His divine mandate.

5. Hope for the Future: The vision of the new heaven and new earth provides hope and assurance of a glorious future under Jesus' eternal reign.

Conclusion

The Book of Revelation vividly portrays the authority of Jesus Christ through powerful imagery and declarations. From His proclamation as the Alpha and Omega to the vision of the glorified Christ, and from the worthy Lamb to the divine judge, Revelation affirms the supreme authority of Jesus over all creation. As we reflect on these truths, we are encouraged to live confidently under His sovereignty, submit to His rule, and engage boldly in His mission. Recognizing the authority of Christ transforms our understanding of His divine nature and our relationship with Him, grounding us in the eternal purpose and love of God.

THE LIFE IN CHRIST

Key Verse: Colossians 3:1-4

Lesson: Since you have been raised with Christ, set your hearts on things above, where Christ is, seated at the right hand of God. Your life is now hidden with Christ in God.

New Life in Christ: An Expository Study in the Book of Revelation

Introduction

The concept of new life in Christ is foundational to Christian faith, emphasizing a transformative relationship with Jesus that changes our focus, priorities, and existence. The Book of Revelation provides rich imagery and profound insights into this new life, illustrating the ultimate destiny and calling of believers. This chapter will explore the lesson of new life in Christ as exhibited in Revelation, using an expository study method with references from Strong's Concordance.

Raised with Christ

Key Verses: Revelation 1:5-6

Revelation affirms the transformative power of Jesus' resurrection, which raises believers to new life and grants them a royal and priestly identity.

- Revelation 1:5-6 (NIV): "To him who loves us and has freed us from our sins by his blood, and has made us to be a kingdom and priests to serve his God and Father—to him be glory and power for ever and ever! Amen."

Expository Insights:

- Freed Us from Our Sins (Strong's G3089): The term "freed" (luo) indicates liberation and release, signifying the new life believers receive through Jesus' sacrifice.

- Kingdom and Priests (Strong's G932 and G2409): Reflects the elevated status and purpose of believers in Christ, who are called to serve God with a royal and priestly role.

- This passage underscores the new identity and mission believers have as a result of being raised with Christ.

Setting Hearts on Things Above

Key Verses: Revelation 3:21

Believers are encouraged to focus on their heavenly calling and the ultimate reward of reigning with Christ.

- Revelation 3:21 (NIV): "To the one who is victorious, I will give the right to sit with me on my throne, just as I was victorious and sat down with my Father on his throne."

Expository Insights:

- Victorious (Strong's G3528): The term "victorious" (nikao) signifies overcoming and conquering, reflecting the perseverance and faithfulness required of believers.

- Sit with Me on My Throne (Strong's G2521): Indicates the privilege and honor of sharing in Christ's reign, emphasizing the eternal perspective and heavenly focus believers should maintain.

- This promise encourages believers to set their hearts on things above, aligning their lives with the eternal reign of Christ.

Hidden with Christ in God

Key Verses: Revelation 7:15-17

The imagery in Revelation 7 portrays the security and intimacy of being hidden with Christ, where believers find refuge and provision in God's presence.

- Revelation 7:15-17 (NIV): "Therefore, 'they are before the throne of God and serve him day and night in his temple; and he who sits on the throne will shelter them with his presence. Never again will they hunger; never again will they thirst. The sun will not beat down on them,' nor any scorching heat. For the Lamb at the center of the throne will be their shepherd; 'he will lead them to springs of living water.' 'And God will wipe away every tear from their eyes.'"

Expository Insights:

- Shelter Them with His Presence (Strong's G4637): The term "shelter" (skenoo) signifies dwelling and protection, illustrating the security found in being hidden with Christ.

- Lamb as Shepherd (Strong's G4165): Depicts Jesus' role in guiding and caring for believers, providing for their needs and leading them to spiritual nourishment.

- This passage highlights the protective and nurturing aspect of being hidden with Christ in God, offering assurance and comfort to believers.

Living a Transformed Life

Key Verses: Revelation 21:3-4

The vision of the new heaven and new earth encapsulates the ultimate transformation and renewal that believers experience in Christ.

- Revelation 21:3-4 (NIV): "And I heard a loud voice from the throne saying, 'Look! God's dwelling place is now among the people, and he will dwell with them. They will be his people, and God himself will be with them and be their God. He will wipe every tear from their eyes. There will be no more death or mourning or crying or pain, for the old order of things has passed away.'"

Expository Insights:

- God's Dwelling Place (Strong's G4637): Emphasizes the intimate and permanent presence of God with His people, reflecting the transformed relationship believers have with Him.

- No More Death or Mourning (Strong's G2288 and G3997): Signifies the complete renewal and eradication of suffering, marking the fulfillment of believers' transformation in Christ.

- This vision inspires believers to live a transformed life, characterized by the hope and assurance of God's eternal presence and the ultimate renewal of all things.

Practical Implications of New Life in Christ

1. Heavenly Focus: Believers are called to set their hearts on things above, prioritizing their heavenly calling and eternal destiny in Christ.

2. Security and Assurance: Understanding that our lives are hidden with Christ in God provides believers with security and assurance, knowing they are protected and cared for by Him.

3. Transformative Living: Embracing the new life in Christ motivates believers to live transformed lives, reflecting the character and priorities of their Savior.

4. Hope and Renewal: The vision of the new heaven and new earth offers believers hope and encouragement, reminding them of the ultimate renewal and restoration promised in Christ.

5. Identity and Mission: Recognizing their new identity as a kingdom and priests empowers believers to serve God faithfully and fulfill their mission in the world.

Conclusion

The Book of Revelation vividly portrays the new life believers have in Christ through powerful imagery and declarations. From being raised with Christ to setting hearts on things above, and from being hidden with Christ in God to living transformed lives, Revelation affirms the transformative power and eternal hope found in Jesus. As we reflect on these truths, we are encouraged to embrace our new life in Christ, live with a heavenly focus, and anticipate the ultimate renewal and restoration promised in Him. Recognizing the new life in Christ transforms our understanding of our identity, mission, and relationship with God, grounding us in the eternal purpose and love of the Savior.

Raised with Christ

Key Verse: Colossians 3:1-4

Lesson: Since you have been raised with Christ, set your hearts on things above, where Christ is, seated at the right hand of God. Your life is now hidden with Christ in God.

Raised with Christ: An Expository Study in the Book of Revelation

Introduction

The concept of being "raised with Christ" speaks to the transformative power of Jesus' resurrection and its profound impact on believers' lives. This transformation affects every aspect of our daily living, urging us to set our hearts on heavenly things and live out our new identity in Christ. The Book of Revelation, with its rich imagery and powerful declarations, provides deep insights into the implications of being raised with Christ. This chapter will explore this theme, using an expository study method with references from Strong's Concordance.

The Resurrection and New Identity

Key Verses: Revelation 1:5-6

Revelation emphasizes the transformative power of Jesus' resurrection, which grants believers a new identity and status as a kingdom and priests.

- Revelation 1:5-6 (NIV): "To him who loves us and has freed us from our sins by his blood, and has made us to be a kingdom and priests to serve his God and Father—to him be glory and power for ever and ever! Amen."

Expository Insights:

- Freed Us from Our Sins (Strong's G3089): The term "freed" (luo) indicates liberation and release, signifying the new life and freedom believers receive through Jesus' resurrection.

- Kingdom and Priests (Strong's G932 and G2409): Reflects the elevated status and purpose of believers in Christ, who are called to serve God with a royal and priestly role.

- This passage underscores the new identity and mission believers have as a result of being raised with Christ.

The Throne of Heaven

Key Verses: Revelation 4:1-4

John's vision of the throne of heaven provides a powerful image of the transformed life believers are called to live, focusing on the heavenly realities and the worship of God.

- Revelation 4:1-4 (NIV): "After this I looked, and there before me was a door standing open in heaven. And the voice I had first heard speaking to me like a trumpet said, 'Come up here, and I will show you what must take place after this.' At once I was in the Spirit, and there before me was a throne in heaven with someone sitting on it. And the one who sat there had the appearance of jasper and ruby. A rainbow that shone like an emerald encircled the throne. Surrounding the throne were twenty-four other thrones, and seated on them were twenty-four elders. They were dressed in white and had crowns of gold on their heads."

Expository Insights:

- Throne in Heaven (Strong's G2362): Symbolizes divine sovereignty and the ultimate reality believers are to focus on.

- Twenty-Four Elders (Strong's G4245): Represent the redeemed people of God, highlighting the community and worship aspects of the transformed life.

- This vision encourages believers to set their hearts on heavenly things, aligning their lives with the eternal worship and sovereignty of God.

Overcoming and Reigning with Christ

Key Verses: Revelation 3:21

Believers are promised the privilege of reigning with Christ, reflecting the transformative power and victory that come with being raised with Him.

- Revelation 3:21 (NIV): "To the one who is victorious, I will give the right to sit with me on my throne, just as I was victorious and sat down with my Father on his throne."

Expository Insights:

- Victorious (Strong's G3528): The term "victorious" (nikao) signifies overcoming and conquering, reflecting the perseverance and faithfulness required of believers.

- Sit with Me on My Throne (Strong's G2521): Indicates the privilege and honor of sharing in Christ's reign, emphasizing the eternal perspective and heavenly focus believers should maintain.

- This promise encourages believers to live victoriously, embracing their new identity and authority in Christ.

The Resurrection and New Creation

Key Verses: Revelation 21:1-4

The vision of the new heaven and new earth encapsulates the ultimate transformation and renewal that believers experience in Christ.

- Revelation 21:1-4 (NIV): "Then I saw 'a new heaven and a new earth,' for the first heaven and the first earth had passed away, and there was no longer any sea. I saw the Holy City, the new Jerusalem, coming down out of heaven from

God, prepared as a bride beautifully dressed for her husband. And I heard a loud voice from the throne saying, 'Look! God's dwelling place is now among the people, and he will dwell with them. They will be his people, and God himself will be with them and be their God. He will wipe every tear from their eyes. There will be no more death or mourning or crying or pain, for the old order of things has passed away.'"

Expository Insights:

- New Heaven and New Earth (Strong's G2537 and G1093): Signify the complete renewal and restoration of creation by Jesus.

- New Jerusalem (Strong's G2419): Represents the redeemed community of God's people, created anew in Christ.

- God's Dwelling Place (Strong's G4637): Emphasizes the intimate and permanent presence of God with His people, reflecting the transformed relationship believers have with Him.

- This vision inspires believers to live a transformed life, characterized by the hope and assurance of God's eternal presence and the ultimate renewal of all things.

Practical Implications of Being Raised with Christ

1. Heavenly Focus: Believers are called to set their hearts on things above, prioritizing their heavenly calling and eternal destiny in Christ.

2. Victory in Daily Life: Understanding the victory achieved through being raised with Christ encourages believers to live victoriously, overcoming challenges and trials with faith.

3. Transformed Relationships: Embracing the new life in Christ transforms relationships, fostering unity, love, and mutual encouragement among believers.

4. Hope and Assurance: The promise of the new heaven and new earth provides believers with hope and assurance, motivating them to persevere through trials and live faithfully.

5. Identity and Mission: Recognizing their new identity as a kingdom and priests empowers believers to serve God faithfully and fulfill their mission in the world.

Conclusion

The Book of Revelation vividly portrays the transformative power of being raised with Christ through powerful imagery and declarations. From the new identity and mission in Revelation 1 to the heavenly focus in Revelation 4, and from the victory and reigning with Christ in Revelation 3 to the ultimate renewal in Revelation 21, Revelation affirms the profound impact of being spiritually resurrected with Jesus. As we reflect on these truths, we are encouraged to embrace our new life in Christ, live with a heavenly focus, and anticipate the ultimate renewal and restoration promised in Him. Recognizing the transformative power of being raised with Christ transforms our understanding of our identity, mission, and relationship with God, grounding us in the eternal purpose and love of the Savior.

Heavenly Focus

Key Verse: Colossians 3:1-4

Lesson: Since you have been raised with Christ, set your hearts on things above, where Christ is, seated at the right hand of God. Your life is now hidden with Christ in God.

Heavenly Focus: An Expository Study in the Book of Revelation

Introduction

The concept of having a heavenly focus is foundational to Christian living. It emphasizes aligning our thoughts, priorities, and actions with the eternal realities of God's kingdom. The Book of Revelation, with its vivid imagery and powerful visions, provides profound insights into the importance of setting our minds on things above. This chapter will explore the theme of heavenly focus as exhibited in Revelation, using an expository study method with references from Strong's Concordance.

The Vision of the Heavenly Throne

Key Verses: Revelation 4:1-4

John's vision of the heavenly throne room offers a glimpse into the eternal realm where God's sovereign rule is the central focus.

- Revelation 4:1-4 (NIV): "After this I looked, and there before me was a door standing open in heaven. And the voice I had first heard speaking to me like a trumpet said, 'Come up here, and I will show you what must take place after this.' At once I was in the Spirit, and there before me was a throne in heaven with someone sitting on it. And the one who sat there had the appearance of jasper and ruby. A rainbow that shone like an emerald encircled the throne. Surrounding the throne were twenty-four other thrones, and seated on them were twenty-four elders. They were dressed in white and had crowns of gold on their heads."

Expository Insights:

- Throne in Heaven (Strong's G2362): Symbolizes God's sovereignty and central authority in the universe.

- Appearance of Jasper and Ruby (Strong's G2393 and G4556): Represent God's glory, purity, and righteousness.

- Rainbow Encircling the Throne (Strong's G2463): Signifies God's covenant faithfulness and mercy.

- Twenty-Four Elders (Strong's G4245): Represent the redeemed people of God, emphasizing the communal and worshipful aspect of heavenly focus.

This vision encourages believers to fix their gaze on God's throne, recognizing His supreme authority and aligning their lives with His divine will.

The Lamb Who Was Slain

Key Verses: Revelation 5:6-14

The depiction of Jesus as the Lamb who was slain highlights the centrality of Christ's sacrifice and its eternal significance.

- Revelation 5:6-7 (NIV): "Then I saw a Lamb, looking as if it had been slain, standing at the center of the throne, encircled by the four living creatures and the elders. The Lamb had seven horns and seven eyes, which are the seven spirits of God sent out into all the earth. He came and took the scroll from the right hand of him who sat on the throne."

Expository Insights:

- Lamb (Strong's G721): Represents Jesus' sacrificial role, emphasizing His redemptive work.

- Seven Horns and Seven Eyes (Strong's G2768 and G3788): Symbolize complete power and perfect knowledge, reflecting the omnipotence and omniscience of Jesus.

- Seven Spirits of God (Strong's G4151): Indicate the fullness of the Holy Spirit, signifying the divine nature of Jesus.

This passage encourages believers to center their lives on Christ's sacrifice, allowing His redemptive work to shape their perspectives, priorities, and actions.

The Multitude Before the Throne

Key Verses: Revelation 7:9-17

The vision of the great multitude before the throne depicts the eternal worship and service of believers in God's presence.

- Revelation 7:9-10 (NIV): "After this I looked, and there before me was a great multitude that no one could count, from every nation, tribe, people and language, standing before the throne and before the Lamb. They were wearing white robes and were holding palm branches in their hands. And they cried out in a loud voice: 'Salvation belongs to our God, who sits on the throne, and to the Lamb.'"

Expository Insights:

- Great Multitude (Strong's G3793): Represents the inclusive and diverse nature of God's redeemed people.

- White Robes (Strong's G4749): Symbolize purity and victory, reflecting the righteousness imparted by Christ.

- Palm Branches (Strong's G5404): Signify celebration and victory, pointing to the triumph of salvation.

This vision inspires believers to adopt a heavenly perspective, recognizing their ultimate destiny in God's presence and living in anticipation of eternal worship and service.

The New Heaven and the New Earth

Key Verses: Revelation 21:1-4

The vision of the new heaven and new earth offers a powerful glimpse into the ultimate fulfillment of God's redemptive plan.

- Revelation 21:1-4 (NIV): "Then I saw 'a new heaven and a new earth,' for the first heaven and the first earth had passed away, and there was no longer any sea. I saw the Holy City, the new Jerusalem, coming down out of heaven from God, prepared as a bride beautifully dressed for her husband. And I heard a loud voice from the throne saying, 'Look! God's dwelling place is now among the people, and he will dwell with them. They will be his people, and God himself will be with them and be their God. He will wipe every tear from their eyes. There will be no more death or mourning or crying or pain, for the old order of things has passed away.'"

Expository Insights:

- New Heaven and New Earth (Strong's G2537 and G1093): Signify the complete renewal and restoration of creation by Jesus.

- New Jerusalem (Strong's G2419): Represents the redeemed community of God's people, created anew in Christ.

- God's Dwelling Place (Strong's G4637): Emphasizes the intimate and eternal relationship between God and His people.

This vision encourages believers to focus on the eternal hope and ultimate restoration promised in Christ, allowing this perspective to shape their daily living.

Practical Implications of a Heavenly Focus

1. Transformed Perspectives: Setting our minds on things above transforms how we view the world, recognizing the temporal nature of earthly pursuits and the eternal significance of our relationship with God.

2. Reordered Priorities: A heavenly focus reorders our priorities, placing God's kingdom and His will at the forefront of our decisions and actions.

3. Renewed Actions: Aligning our lives with heavenly realities leads to actions that reflect Christ's character, including love, service, and worship.

4. Perseverance and Hope: A heavenly focus provides perseverance and hope in the face of trials, knowing that our ultimate destiny is secure in Christ.

5. Unity and Worship: Recognizing our eternal destiny fosters unity and collective worship among believers, encouraging us to live in harmony and anticipation of eternal fellowship with God.

Conclusion

The Book of Revelation vividly portrays the importance of having a heavenly focus through powerful imagery and declarations. From the vision of the heavenly throne to the depiction of the Lamb who was slain, and from the multitude before the throne to the ultimate fulfillment in the new heaven and new earth, Revelation affirms the transformative impact of setting our minds on things above. As we reflect on these truths, we are encouraged to embrace a heavenly focus, allowing it to transform our perspectives, reorder our priorities, and renew our actions. Recognizing the significance of a heavenly focus transforms our understanding of our identity, mission, and relationship with God, grounding us in the eternal purpose and love of the Savior.

Hidden with Christ

Key Verse: Colossians 3:1-4

Lesson: Since you have been raised with Christ, set your hearts on things above, where Christ is, seated at the right hand of God. Your life is now hidden with Christ in God.

Hidden with Christ: An Expository Study in the Book of Revelation

Introduction

The concept of being "hidden with Christ in God" conveys a profound sense of security and identity for believers. It emphasizes our union with Christ, the protection we have in Him, and the new identity we possess as His followers. The Book of Revelation offers vivid imagery and deep insights into this theme, illustrating the ultimate security and identity believers find in Christ. This chapter will explore the theme of being hidden with Christ as exhibited in Revelation, using an expository study method with references from Strong's Concordance.

Security in Christ's Presence

Key Verses: Revelation 1:12-18

The initial vision of Christ in Revelation provides a powerful image of His presence among the churches, symbolizing security and guidance.

- Revelation 1:12-18 (NIV): "I turned around to see the voice that was speaking to me. And when I turned I saw seven golden lampstands, and among the lampstands was someone like a son of man, dressed in a robe reaching down to his feet and with a golden sash around his chest. The hair on his head was white like wool, as white as snow, and his eyes were like blazing fire. His feet were like bronze glowing in a furnace, and his voice was like the sound of rushing waters. In his right hand he held seven stars, and coming out of his mouth was a sharp, double-edged sword. His face was like the sun shining in all its brilliance."

Expository Insights:

- Seven Golden Lampstands (Strong's G3087): Represent the seven churches, indicating Christ's presence among His people.

- Son of Man (Strong's G5207 and G444): A title emphasizing Jesus' humanity and divinity.

- Seven Stars (Strong's G792): Symbolize the angels of the seven churches, showing Jesus' control and care over the church's leadership and direction.

- Voice Like Rushing Waters (Strong's G5456): Emphasizes the power and authority of His words.

This vision assures believers of the security found in Christ's presence, knowing that He is among His people, guiding and protecting them.

Identity in Christ's Victory

Key Verses: Revelation 3:12

The promise to the victorious believers in Philadelphia highlights the new identity and security they have in Christ.

- Revelation 3:12 (NIV): "The one who is victorious I will make a pillar in the temple of my God. Never again will they leave it. I will write on them the name of my God and the name of the city of my God, the new Jerusalem, which is coming down out of heaven from my God; and I will also write on them my new name."

Expository Insights:

- Pillar in the Temple (Strong's G4769): Symbolizes stability, permanence, and honor in God's presence.

- Name of My God (Strong's G3686): Signifies belonging and identity, reflecting a personal relationship with God.

- New Jerusalem (Strong's G2419): Represents the redeemed community of God's people, emphasizing their new identity in Christ.

This promise underscores the new identity and eternal security believers have in Christ, marked by a personal relationship with God and a permanent place in His kingdom.

Protection Under Christ's Reign

Key Verses: Revelation 7:15-17

The vision of the multitude before the throne provides a powerful image of the protection and provision found in Christ.

- Revelation 7:15-17 (NIV): "Therefore, 'they are before the throne of God and serve him day and night in his temple; and he who sits on the throne will shelter them with his presence. Never again will they hunger; never again will they thirst. The sun will not beat down on them,' nor any scorching heat. For the Lamb at the center of the throne will be their shepherd; 'he will lead them to springs of living water.' 'And God will wipe away every tear from their eyes.'"

Expository Insights:

- Shelter Them with His Presence (Strong's G4637): The term "shelter" (skenoo) signifies dwelling and protection, illustrating the security found in being hidden with Christ.

- Lamb as Shepherd (Strong's G4165): Depicts Jesus' role in guiding and caring for believers, providing for their needs and leading them to spiritual nourishment.

- Wipe Away Every Tear (Strong's G1813): Symbolizes comfort and the removal of suffering, emphasizing the care and compassion of Christ.

This vision highlights the protective and nurturing aspect of being hidden with Christ, offering assurance and comfort to believers.

Eternal Security in the New Creation

Key Verses: Revelation 21:1-4

The vision of the new heaven and new earth encapsulates the ultimate security and identity believers find in Christ.

- Revelation 21:1-4 (NIV): "Then I saw 'a new heaven and a new earth,' for the first heaven and the first earth had passed away, and there was no longer any sea. I saw the Holy City, the new Jerusalem, coming down out of heaven from God, prepared as a bride beautifully dressed for her husband. And I heard a loud voice from the throne saying, 'Look! God's dwelling place is now among the people, and he will dwell with them. They will be his people, and God himself will be with them and be their God. He will wipe every tear from their eyes. There will be no more death or mourning or crying or pain, for the old order of things has passed away.'"

Expository Insights:

- New Heaven and New Earth (Strong's G2537 and G1093): Signify the complete renewal and restoration of creation by Jesus.

- New Jerusalem (Strong's G2419): Represents the redeemed community of God's people, created anew in Christ.

- God's Dwelling Place (Strong's G4637): Emphasizes the intimate and eternal relationship between God and His people.

This vision encourages believers to find their ultimate security and identity in the eternal reality of the new creation, where they will dwell with God forever.

Practical Implications of Being Hidden with Christ

1. Security in Christ: Believers can live confidently, knowing they are secure in Christ's presence and protection.

2. New Identity: Understanding their identity in Christ empowers believers to live out their new status as children of God, marked by His name and belonging to His kingdom.

3. Eternal Perspective: Embracing the eternal security promised in the new creation encourages believers to live with hope and assurance, focusing on their ultimate destiny with God.

4. Daily Dependence: Recognizing the protective and nurturing role of Christ as Shepherd leads believers to rely on His guidance and provision in their daily lives.

5. Comfort in Trials: The promise of God's comfort and the removal of suffering provides encouragement and strength in the face of trials and challenges.

Conclusion

The Book of Revelation vividly portrays the security and identity believers find in being hidden with Christ through powerful imagery and declarations. From the vision of Christ among the churches to the promise of eternal security in the new creation, Revelation affirms the profound sense of belonging and protection that comes from being united with Christ. As we reflect on these truths, we are encouraged to embrace our identity in Christ, live confidently in His protection, and anticipate the ultimate fulfillment of God's promises. Recognizing the security and identity found in being hidden with Christ transforms our understanding of our relationship with God, grounding us in His eternal purpose and love.

CHAPTER 04

CHRIST, THE HEAD OF THE CHURCH

Key Verse: Colossians 1:18

Lesson: He is the head of the body, the church; He is the beginning and the firstborn from among the dead, so that in everything He might have the supremacy.

Christ, the Head of the Church: An Expository Study in the Book of Revelation

Introduction

The concept of Christ as the head of the church is central to understanding the relationship between Jesus and His followers. It emphasizes His supreme authority, leadership, and the vital connection between Him and His body, the church. The Book of Revelation offers profound insights into this theme, illustrating Christ's role and supremacy over the church. This chapter will explore the lesson of Christ as the head of the church as exhibited in Revelation, using an expository study method with references from Strong's Concordance.

The Vision of Christ among the Lampstands

Key Verses: Revelation 1:12-20

John's vision of Christ among the seven golden lampstands provides a powerful image of Jesus' presence and authority within the church.

- Revelation 1:12-13 (NIV): "I turned around to see the voice that was speaking to me. And when I turned I saw seven golden lampstands, and among the lampstands was someone like a son of man, dressed in a robe reaching down to his feet and with a golden sash around his chest."

Expository Insights:

- Seven Golden Lampstands (Strong's G3087): Represent the seven churches, indicating Christ's presence and authority among His people.

- Son of Man (Strong's G5207 and G444): A title emphasizing Jesus' humanity and divinity, rooted in Daniel 7:13-14.

Key Verses: Revelation 1:17-18

- Revelation 1:17-18 (NIV): "When I saw him, I fell at his feet as though dead. Then he placed his right hand on me and said: 'Do not be afraid. I am the First and the Last. I am the Living One; I was dead, and now look, I am alive for ever and ever! And I hold the keys of death and Hades.'"

Expository Insights:

- First and the Last (Strong's G4413 and G2078): Indicate Jesus' eternal nature and authority over all time.

- Living One (Strong's G2198): Emphasizes His resurrection and eternal life.

- Keys of Death and Hades (Strong's G2807, G2288, and G86): Symbolize His authority over life, death, and the afterlife.

This vision underscores Christ's supreme authority and His role as the living and active head of the church, guiding, protecting, and leading His people.

Messages to the Seven Churches

Key Verses: Revelation 2-3

The messages to the seven churches reveal Christ's intimate knowledge of each congregation, His authority to commend and correct, and His role in guiding the church toward faithfulness.

Church of Ephesus:

- Revelation 2:1 (NIV): "To the angel of the church in Ephesus write: These are the words of him who holds the seven stars in his right hand and walks among the seven golden lampstands."

Expository Insights:

- Holds the Seven Stars (Strong's G2902): Indicates Christ's control and authority over the church's leaders.

- Walks among the Seven Golden Lampstands (Strong's G4043 and G3087): Emphasizes His active presence and oversight within the church.

Church of Smyrna:

- Revelation 2:8 (NIV): "To the angel of the church in Smyrna write: These are the words of him who is the First and the Last, who died and came to life again."

Expository Insights:

- First and the Last (Strong's G4413 and G2078): Reinforces Christ's eternal authority.

- Died and Came to Life Again (Strong's G599 and G2198): Highlights His victory over death and His power to grant eternal life.

Each message demonstrates Christ's deep care and authoritative leadership, correcting, encouraging, and directing the church according to His divine wisdom and purpose.

Christ's Supremacy and the New Creation

Key Verses: Revelation 21:5-7

The vision of the new heaven and new earth emphasizes Christ's role in bringing about the ultimate renewal of creation and His supreme authority in the new order.

- Revelation 21:5-7 (NIV): "He who was seated on the throne said, 'I am making everything new!' Then he said, 'Write this down, for these words are trustworthy and true.' He said to me: 'It is done. I am the Alpha and the Omega, the Beginning and the End. To the thirsty I will give water without cost from the spring of the water of life. Those who are victorious will inherit all this, and I will be their God and they will be my children.'"

Expository Insights:

- Making Everything New (Strong's G2537): Signifies Christ's authority to renew and restore all creation.

- Alpha and Omega (Strong's G1 and G5598): Indicate Jesus' eternal and encompassing authority.

- Spring of the Water of Life (Strong's G4077): Represents the eternal life and sustenance Christ provides.

This vision affirms Christ's supreme authority over the new creation, underscoring His role as the head who brings about the ultimate renewal and fulfillment of God's plan.

The Lamb and the Redeemed

Key Verses: Revelation 7:9-17

The vision of the multitude before the throne highlights the unity and worship of the redeemed, led and sustained by Christ.

- Revelation 7:17 (NIV): "For the Lamb at the center of the throne will be their shepherd; 'he will lead them to springs of living water.' 'And God will wipe away every tear from their eyes.'"

Expository Insights:

- Lamb at the Center of the Throne (Strong's G721 and G2362): Emphasizes Christ's central role and authority in the eternal kingdom.

- Shepherd (Strong's G4165): Indicates His role in guiding, protecting, and providing for His people.

- Springs of Living Water (Strong's G4077): Symbolizes the eternal life and nourishment Christ offers.

This vision illustrates the unity of the redeemed under Christ's leadership and the eternal provision and comfort He provides as their head.

Practical Implications of Christ as Head of the Church

1. Authority and Guidance: Recognizing Christ as the head of the church calls believers to submit to His authority and follow His guidance in all aspects of life.

2. Unity and Community: Understanding the church as Christ's body fosters unity and mutual care among believers, as each member is connected to Christ and one another.

3. Mission and Purpose: Embracing Christ's leadership empowers the church to fulfill its mission and purpose, advancing His kingdom on earth.

4. Hope and Assurance: Knowing Christ's supreme authority and eternal reign provides believers with hope and assurance, even in the face of trials and challenges.

5. Worship and Devotion: Acknowledging Christ as the head of the church inspires worship and devotion, as believers honor Him for His sacrificial love and sovereign rule.

Conclusion

The Book of Revelation vividly portrays Christ's role as the head of the church through powerful imagery and declarations. From the vision of Christ among the lampstands to the messages to the seven churches, and from the vision of the new creation to the unity of the redeemed, Revelation affirms Christ's supreme authority and leadership over His people. As we reflect on these truths, we are encouraged to submit to Christ's authority, embrace our identity as His body, and live out His mission with hope and assurance. Recognizing Christ as the head of the church transforms our understanding of our relationship with Him and our role in His kingdom, grounding us in His eternal purpose and love.

Jesus as Head

Key Verse: Colossians 1:18

Lesson: He is the head of the body, the church; He is the beginning and the firstborn from among the dead, so that in everything He might have the supremacy.

Jesus as Head: An Expository Study in the Book of Revelation

Introduction

Understanding Jesus as the head of the church is vital to comprehending the relationship between Christ and His followers. This role emphasizes His supreme authority, guidance, nurturing care, and leadership. The Book of Revelation, with its rich and vivid imagery, offers profound insights into Jesus' role as the head of the church. This chapter will explore the theme of Jesus as head as exhibited in Revelation, using an expository study method with references from Strong's Concordance.

The Vision of Christ among the Lampstands

Key Verses: Revelation 1:12-20

John's vision of Christ among the seven golden lampstands provides a powerful image of Jesus' presence and authority within the church.

- Revelation 1:12-13 (NIV): "I turned around to see the voice that was speaking to me. And when I turned I saw seven golden lampstands, and among the lampstands was someone like a son of man, dressed in a robe reaching down to his feet and with a golden sash around his chest."

Expository Insights:

- Seven Golden Lampstands (Strong's G3087): Represent the seven churches, indicating Christ's presence among His people.

- Son of Man (Strong's G5207 and G444): A title emphasizing Jesus' humanity and divinity, rooted in Daniel 7:13-14.

Key Verses: Revelation 1:17-18

- Revelation 1:17-18 (NIV): "When I saw him, I fell at his feet as though dead. Then he placed his right hand on me and said: 'Do not be afraid. I am the First and the Last. I am the Living One; I was dead, and now look, I am alive for ever and ever! And I hold the keys of death and Hades.'"

Expository Insights:

- First and the Last (Strong's G4413 and G2078): Indicate Jesus' eternal nature and authority over all time.

- Living One (Strong's G2198): Emphasizes His resurrection and eternal life.

- Keys of Death and Hades (Strong's G2807, G2288, and G86): Symbolize His authority over life, death, and the afterlife.

This vision underscores Christ's supreme authority and His role as the living and active head of the church, guiding, protecting, and leading His people.

Messages to the Seven Churches

Key Verses: Revelation 2-3

The messages to the seven churches reveal Christ's intimate knowledge of each congregation, His authority to commend and correct, and His role in guiding the church toward faithfulness.

Church of Ephesus:

- Revelation 2:1 (NIV): "To the angel of the church in Ephesus write: These are the words of him who holds the seven stars in his right hand and walks among the seven golden lampstands."

Expository Insights:

- Holds the Seven Stars (Strong's G2902): Indicates Christ's control and authority over the church's leaders.

- Walks among the Seven Golden Lampstands (Strong's G4043 and G3087): Emphasizes His active presence and oversight within the church.

Church of Smyrna:

- Revelation 2:8 (NIV): "To the angel of the church in Smyrna write: These are the words of him who is the First and the Last, who died and came to life again."

Expository Insights:

- First and the Last (Strong's G4413 and G2078): Reinforces Christ's eternal authority.

- Died and Came to Life Again (Strong's G599 and G2198): Highlights His victory over death and His power to grant eternal life.

Each message demonstrates Christ's deep care and authoritative leadership, correcting, encouraging, and directing the church according to His divine wisdom and purpose.

The Lamb and the Redeemed

Key Verses: Revelation 5:6-14

The depiction of Jesus as the Lamb who was slain highlights His central role in redemption and His authority over the church.

- Revelation 5:6-7 (NIV): "Then I saw a Lamb, looking as if it had been slain, standing at the center of the throne, encircled by the four living creatures and the elders. The Lamb had seven horns and seven eyes, which are the seven spirits of God sent out into all the earth. He came and took the scroll from the right hand of him who sat on the throne."

Expository Insights:

- Lamb (Strong's G721): Represents Jesus' sacrificial role, emphasizing His redemptive work.

- Seven Horns and Seven Eyes (Strong's G2768 and G3788): Symbolize complete power and perfect knowledge, underscoring Jesus' omnipotence and omniscience.

- Seven Spirits of God (Strong's G4151): Indicate the fullness of the Holy Spirit, reflecting the divine nature of Jesus.

This passage emphasizes Christ's central role in the redemption of humanity and His authoritative position within the church, guiding and empowering His followers.

Christ's Supremacy and the New Creation

Key Verses: Revelation 21:5-7

The vision of the new heaven and new earth emphasizes Christ's role in bringing about the ultimate renewal of creation and His supreme authority in the new order.

- Revelation 21:5-7 (NIV): "He who was seated on the throne said, 'I am making everything new!' Then he said,

'Write this down, for these words are trustworthy and true.'
He said to me: 'It is done. I am the Alpha and the Omega, the
Beginning and the End. To the thirsty I will give water
without cost from the spring of the water of life. Those who
are victorious will inherit all this, and I will be their God and
they will be my children.'"

Expository Insights:

- Making Everything New (Strong's G2537): Signifies
Christ's authority to renew and restore all creation.

- Alpha and Omega (Strong's G1 and G5598): Indicate
Jesus' eternal and encompassing authority.

- Spring of the Water of Life (Strong's G4077):
Represents the eternal life and sustenance Christ provides.

This vision affirms Christ's supreme authority over
the new creation, underscoring His role as the head who
brings about the ultimate renewal and fulfillment of God's
plan.

Practical Implications of Jesus as Head

1. Authority and Guidance: Recognizing Jesus as the
head of the church calls believers to submit to His authority
and follow His guidance in all aspects of life.

2. Unity and Community: Understanding the church
as Christ's body fosters unity and mutual care among

believers, as each member is connected to Christ and one another.

3. Mission and Purpose: Embracing Christ's leadership empowers the church to fulfill its mission and purpose, advancing His kingdom on earth.

4. Hope and Assurance: Knowing Christ's supreme authority and eternal reign provides believers with hope and assurance, even in the face of trials and challenges.

5. Worship and Devotion: Acknowledging Christ as the head of the church inspires worship and devotion, as believers honor Him for His sacrificial love and sovereign rule.

Conclusion

The Book of Revelation vividly portrays Jesus' role as the head of the church through powerful imagery and declarations. From the vision of Christ among the lampstands to the messages to the seven churches, and from the vision of the new creation to the unity of the redeemed, Revelation affirms Christ's supreme authority and leadership over His people. As we reflect on these truths, we are encouraged to submit to Christ's authority, embrace our identity as His body, and live out His mission with hope and assurance. Recognizing Jesus as the head of the church transforms our understanding of our relationship with Him and our role in His kingdom, grounding us in His eternal purpose and love.

Resurrection Hope

Key Verse: Colossians 1:18

Lesson: He is the head of the body, the church; He is the beginning and the firstborn from among the dead, so that in everything He might have the supremacy.

Resurrection Hope: An Expository Study in the Book of Revelation

Introduction

The resurrection of Jesus Christ is a cornerstone of Christian faith, providing the ultimate hope and assurance of our future resurrection. As the firstborn from the dead, Jesus' resurrection guarantees the future resurrection of all who believe in Him. The Book of Revelation powerfully depicts this hope through its vivid imagery and profound declarations. This chapter will explore the theme of resurrection hope as exhibited in Revelation, using an expository study method with references from Strong's Concordance.

Jesus, the Living One

Key Verses: Revelation 1:17-18

John's vision of the risen Christ emphasizes Jesus' eternal life and authority over death, offering believers hope in His resurrection.

- Revelation 1:17-18 (NIV): "When I saw him, I fell at his feet as though dead. Then he placed his right hand on me and said: 'Do not be afraid. I am the First and the Last. I am the Living One; I was dead, and now look, I am alive for ever and ever! And I hold the keys of death and Hades.'"

Expository Insights:

- First and the Last (Strong's G4413 and G2078): Indicate Jesus' eternal nature and authority over all time.

- Living One (Strong's G2198): Emphasizes His resurrection and eternal life.

- Keys of Death and Hades (Strong's G2807, G2288, and G86): Symbolize His authority over life, death, and the afterlife.

This vision underscores the hope and assurance believers have in Jesus' victory over death, promising eternal life to all who trust in Him.

The Multitude Before the Throne

Key Verses: Revelation 7:9-17

The vision of the great multitude before the throne illustrates the fulfillment of the resurrection hope, as believers from all nations stand redeemed and victorious in God's presence.

- Revelation 7:9-10 (NIV): "After this I looked, and there before me was a great multitude that no one could count, from every nation, tribe, people and language, standing before the throne and before the Lamb. They were wearing white robes and were holding palm branches in their hands. And they cried out in a loud voice: 'Salvation belongs to our God, who sits on the throne, and to the Lamb.'"

Expository Insights:

- Great Multitude (Strong's G3793): Represents the inclusive and diverse nature of God's redeemed people.

- White Robes (Strong's G4749): Symbolize purity and victory, reflecting the righteousness imparted by Christ.

- Palm Branches (Strong's G5404): Signify celebration and victory, pointing to the triumph of salvation.

This vision highlights the ultimate realization of resurrection hope, with believers gathered in eternal worship and victory before God's throne.

The First Resurrection

Key Verses: Revelation 20:4-6

The passage describing the first resurrection provides insight into the blessedness and hope of those who partake in the resurrection life through Christ.

- Revelation 20:4-6 (NIV): "I saw thrones on which were seated those who had been given authority to judge. And I saw the souls of those who had been beheaded because of their testimony about Jesus and because of the word of God. They had not worshiped the beast or its image and had not received its mark on their foreheads or their hands. They came to life and reigned with Christ a thousand years. (The rest of the dead did not come to life until the thousand years were ended.) This is the first resurrection. Blessed and holy are those who share in the first resurrection. The second death has no power over them, but they will be priests of God and of Christ and will reign with him for a thousand years."

Expository Insights:

- First Resurrection (Strong's G386 and G4413): Refers to the initial raising of the dead in Christ, signifying the blessedness of eternal life with God.

- Blessed and Holy (Strong's G3107 and G40): Indicates the privileged and sanctified status of those who share in this resurrection.

- Second Death (Strong's G1208 and G2288): Represents eternal separation from God, which has no power over those who are in Christ.

This passage emphasizes the hope and assurance of participating in the first resurrection, promising eternal life and reign with Christ.

The New Heaven and the New Earth

Key Verses: Revelation 21:1-4

The vision of the new heaven and new earth encapsulates the ultimate fulfillment of resurrection hope, where believers experience eternal life in the renewed creation.

- Revelation 21:1-4 (NIV): "Then I saw 'a new heaven and a new earth,' for the first heaven and the first earth had passed away, and there was no longer any sea. I saw the Holy City, the new Jerusalem, coming down out of heaven from God, prepared as a bride beautifully dressed for her husband. And I heard a loud voice from the throne saying, 'Look! God's dwelling place is now among the people, and he will dwell with them. They will be his people, and God himself will be with them and be their God. He will wipe every tear from their eyes. There will be no more death or mourning or crying or pain, for the old order of things has passed away.'"

Expository Insights:

- New Heaven and New Earth (Strong's G2537 and G1093): Signify the complete renewal and restoration of creation by Jesus.

- New Jerusalem (Strong's G2419): Represents the redeemed community of God's people, created anew in Christ.

- God's Dwelling Place (Strong's G4637): Emphasizes the intimate and eternal relationship between God and His people.

This vision offers a powerful picture of the resurrection hope, where believers enjoy eternal life, free from death and suffering, in the presence of God.

Practical Implications of Resurrection Hope

1. Assurance of Eternal Life: The resurrection of Jesus guarantees the future resurrection of believers, providing assurance of eternal life with God.

2. Victory Over Death: Understanding the hope of resurrection empowers believers to live victoriously, unafraid of death and confident in Christ's triumph.

3. Motivation for Faithfulness: The promise of resurrection hope encourages believers to remain faithful, even in the face of persecution and trials, knowing their ultimate reward is secure.

4. Comfort in Grief: The assurance of resurrection offers comfort and hope in times of loss, reminding believers that death is not the end for those in Christ.

5. Focus on Eternal Promises: Embracing resurrection hope shifts believers' focus from temporary, earthly concerns to the eternal promises of God, inspiring them to live with purpose and expectation.

Conclusion

The Book of Revelation vividly portrays the hope and assurance of resurrection through powerful imagery and declarations. From the vision of the risen Christ to the multitude before the throne, and from the description of the first resurrection to the ultimate fulfillment in the new heaven and new earth, Revelation affirms the profound hope believers have in Jesus' resurrection. As we reflect on these truths, we are encouraged to embrace the assurance of eternal life, live victoriously, remain faithful, find comfort in times of grief, and focus on God's eternal promises. Recognizing the significance of Jesus as the firstborn from the dead transforms our understanding of our future resurrection, grounding us in the eternal purpose and love of God.

Supremacy of Christ

Key Verse: Colossians 1:18

Lesson: He is the head of the body, the church; He is the beginning and the firstborn from among the dead, so that in everything He might have the supremacy.

Supremacy of Christ: An Expository Study in the Book of Revelation

Introduction

The supremacy of Christ is a fundamental theme in Christian theology, emphasizing His ultimate authority, preeminence, and sovereign rule over all creation. The Book of Revelation powerfully illustrates this supremacy through its vivid imagery and profound declarations. This chapter will explore the theme of Christ's supremacy as exhibited in Revelation, using an expository study method with references from Strong's Concordance. By understanding Jesus' supreme position, we can better align our worship, obedience, and devotion to Him.

The Vision of the Glorified Christ

Key Verses: Revelation 1:12-18

John's initial vision of the glorified Christ sets the stage for understanding His supreme authority and divine majesty.

- Revelation 1:12-18 (NIV): "I turned around to see the voice that was speaking to me. And when I turned I saw seven golden lampstands, and among the lampstands was someone like a son of man, dressed in a robe reaching down to his feet and with a golden sash around his chest. The hair on his head was white like wool, as white as snow, and his eyes were like blazing fire. His feet were like bronze glowing in a furnace, and his voice was like the sound of rushing waters. In his right hand he held seven stars, and coming out of his mouth was a sharp, double-edged sword. His face was like the sun shining in all its brilliance."

Expository Insights:

- Seven Golden Lampstands (Strong's G3087): Represent the seven churches, indicating Christ's presence and authority among His people.

- Son of Man (Strong's G5207 and G444): A title emphasizing Jesus' humanity and divinity, rooted in Daniel 7:13-14.

- White Hair (Strong's G3022): Symbolizes purity, holiness, and eternal wisdom.

- Blazing Eyes (Strong's G3788): Denote His penetrating vision and omniscience.

- Glowing Feet (Strong's G5474): Represent judgment and strength.

- Voice Like Rushing Waters (Strong's G5456): Emphasizes the power and authority of His words.

- Double-edged Sword (Strong's G4501): Symbolizes the discerning and powerful nature of His word.

- Face Like the Sun (Strong's G2246): Reflects His divine glory and brilliance.

This vision underscores Christ's supreme authority, encouraging believers to respond with reverence, worship, and obedience.

The Throne Room Vision

Key Verses: Revelation 4:1-11

John's vision of the heavenly throne room provides a majestic depiction of Christ's supremacy and the worship He receives in heaven.

- Revelation 4:1-11 (NIV): "After this I looked, and there before me was a door standing open in heaven. And the voice I had first heard speaking to me like a trumpet said, 'Come up here, and I will show you what must take place after this.' At once I was in the Spirit, and there before me was a throne in heaven with someone sitting on it. And the one who sat there had the appearance of jasper and ruby. A rainbow that shone like an emerald encircled the throne. Surrounding the throne were twenty-four other thrones, and seated on them were twenty-four elders. They were dressed in white and had crowns of gold on their heads. From the throne came flashes of lightning, rumblings, and peals of thunder. In front of the throne, seven lamps were blazing. These are the seven spirits of God. Also in front of the throne there was what looked like a sea of glass, clear as crystal."

Expository Insights:

- Throne in Heaven (Strong's G2362): Symbolizes divine sovereignty and the central authority of Christ.

- Jasper and Ruby (Strong's G2393 and G4556): Represent God's glory, purity, and righteous judgment.

- Rainbow (Strong's G2463): Signifies God's covenant faithfulness.

- Twenty-Four Elders (Strong's G4245): Represent the redeemed people of God, emphasizing communal worship.

- Flashes of Lightning and Thunder (Strong's G796 and G1027): Indicate the power and majesty of God's throne.

- Seven Lamps (Strong's G2985): Represent the fullness of the Holy Spirit.

The heavenly worship scene emphasizes Christ's supreme position, inviting believers to participate in wholehearted worship and adoration.

The Worthy Lamb

Key Verses: Revelation 5:6-14

The depiction of Jesus as the Lamb who was slain highlights His worthiness and supreme authority to execute God's redemptive plan.

- Revelation 5:6-7 (NIV): "Then I saw a Lamb, looking as if it had been slain, standing at the center of the throne, encircled by the four living creatures and the elders. The Lamb had seven horns and seven eyes, which are the seven spirits of God sent out into all the earth. He came and took the scroll from the right hand of him who sat on the throne."

Expository Insights:

- Lamb (Strong's G721): Represents Jesus' sacrificial role, emphasizing His redemptive work.

- Seven Horns and Seven Eyes (Strong's G2768 and G3788): Symbolize complete power and perfect knowledge, underscoring Jesus' omnipotence and omniscience.

- Seven Spirits of God (Strong's G4151): Indicate the fullness of the Holy Spirit, reflecting the divine nature of Jesus.

Key Verses: Revelation 5:9-10

- Revelation 5:9-10 (NIV): "And they sang a new song, saying: 'You are worthy to take the scroll and to open its seals, because you were slain, and with your blood you purchased for God persons from every tribe and language and people and nation. You have made them to be a kingdom and priests to serve our God, and they will reign on the earth.'"

Expository Insights:

- Worthy (Strong's G514): Denotes deserving honor and reverence.

- Purchased for God (Strong's G59): Emphasizes the redemptive price paid by Christ's sacrifice.

- Kingdom and Priests (Strong's G932 and G2409): Reflects the new identity and mission of the redeemed.

This passage reinforces Christ's supreme worthiness and authority, calling believers to respond with devotion and service.

The King of Kings and Lord of Lords

Key Verses: Revelation 19:11-16

In Revelation 19, Jesus is portrayed as the victorious King of Kings and Lord of Lords, emphasizing His ultimate authority over all creation.

- Revelation 19:11-16 (NIV): "I saw heaven standing open and there before me was a white horse, whose rider is called Faithful and True. With justice he judges and wages war. His eyes are like blazing fire, and on his head are many crowns. He has a name written on him that no one knows but he himself. He is dressed in a robe dipped in blood, and his name is the Word of God. The armies of heaven were following him, riding on white horses and dressed in fine linen, white and clean. Coming out of his mouth is a sharp sword with which to strike down the nations. 'He will rule them with an iron scepter.' He treads the winepress of the fury of the wrath of God Almighty. On his robe and on his thigh he has this name written: KING OF KINGS AND LORD OF LORDS."

Expository Insights:

- White Horse (Strong's G3022): Symbolizes victory and purity.

- Faithful and True (Strong's G4103 and G228): Titles that emphasize Jesus' reliability and integrity.

- Many Crowns (Strong's G1238): Represent His supreme authority over all realms.

- Word of God (Strong's G3056): Highlights Jesus' role as the divine Logos.

- Iron Scepter (Strong's G4464): Symbolizes His unyielding rule and judgment.

- King of Kings and Lord of Lords (Strong's G935 and G2962): Titles that affirm His ultimate supremacy.

This portrayal of Jesus as the victorious King calls believers to recognize His supreme authority and to live in obedience to His righteous rule.

The New Heaven and the New Earth

Key Verses: Revelation 21:1-7

The vision of the new heaven and new earth encapsulates the ultimate realization of Christ's supremacy in the renewed creation.

- Revelation 21:1-4 (NIV): "Then I saw 'a new heaven and a new earth,' for the first heaven and the first earth had passed away, and there was no longer any sea. I saw the Holy

City, the new Jerusalem, coming down out of heaven from God, prepared as a bride beautifully dressed for her husband. And I heard a loud voice from the throne saying, 'Look! God's dwelling place is now among the people, and he will dwell with them. They will be his people, and God himself will be with them and be their God. He will wipe every tear from their eyes. There will be no more death or mourning or crying or pain, for the old order of things has passed away.'"

Expository Insights:

- New Heaven and New Earth (Strong's G2537 and G1093): Signify the complete renewal and restoration of creation by Jesus.

- New Jerusalem (Strong's G2419): Represents the redeemed community of God's people, created anew in Christ.

- God's Dwelling Place (Strong's G4637): Emphasizes the intimate and eternal relationship between God and His people.

This vision affirms the ultimate supremacy of Christ in the new creation, inspiring believers to live in anticipation of His eternal reign.

Practical Implications of the Supremacy of Christ

1. Worship: Recognizing Christ's supremacy calls believers to offer wholehearted worship, acknowledging His ultimate authority and worthiness.

2. Obedience: Understanding Jesus' supreme position compels believers to live in obedience to His commands, aligning their lives with His will.

3. Devotion: Embracing Christ's supremacy inspires deep devotion and commitment to Him, prioritizing His kingdom above all else.

4. Hope: The assurance of Christ's ultimate victory and reign provides believers with hope and encouragement, even in the face of trials.

5. Unity: Acknowledging Christ as supreme fosters unity within the church, as all believers are united under His headship.

Conclusion

The Book of Revelation vividly portrays the supremacy of Christ through powerful imagery and declarations. From the vision of the glorified Christ to the heavenly throne room, and from the worthy Lamb to the victorious King of Kings, Revelation affirms Jesus' ultimate authority and preeminence. As we reflect on these truths, we are encouraged to respond with worship, obedience, and devotion, recognizing Christ's supreme position in our lives and in all creation. Embracing the supremacy of Christ transforms our understanding of our relationship with Him and our role in His kingdom, grounding us in His eternal purpose and love.

CHAPTER 05

RECONCILIATION THROUGH CHRIST

Key Verse: Colossians 1:19-20

Lesson: For God was pleased to have all His fullness dwell in Him, and through Him to reconcile to Himself all things, whether things on earth or things in heaven, by making peace through His blood, shed on the cross.

Reconciliation Through Christ: An Expository Study in the Book of Revelation

Introduction

Reconciliation through Christ is a central theme in Christian theology, highlighting how Jesus' sacrificial death on the cross restores the broken relationship between God and humanity. The Book of Revelation, with its vivid imagery and profound declarations, powerfully illustrates the reconciliation that Christ brings. This chapter will explore the theme of reconciliation through Christ as exhibited in Revelation, using an expository study method with references from Strong's Concordance.

The Lamb Who Was Slain

Key Verses: Revelation 5:6-10

The depiction of Jesus as the Lamb who was slain emphasizes His role in reconciliation and redemption.

- Revelation 5:6-10 (NIV): "Then I saw a Lamb, looking as if it had been slain, standing at the center of the throne, encircled by the four living creatures and the elders. The Lamb had seven horns and seven eyes, which are the seven spirits of God sent out into all the earth. He went and took the scroll from the right hand of him who sat on the throne. And when he had taken it, the four living creatures and the twenty-four elders fell down before the Lamb. Each one had a harp and they were holding golden bowls full of incense, which are the prayers of God's people. And they sang a new song, saying: 'You are worthy to take the scroll and to open its seals, because you were slain, and with your blood you purchased for God persons from every tribe and language and people and nation. You have made them to be a kingdom and priests to serve our God, and they will reign on the earth.'"

Expository Insights:

- Lamb (Strong's G721): Represents Jesus' sacrificial role, emphasizing His redemptive work.

- Seven Horns and Seven Eyes (Strong's G2768 and G3788): Symbolize complete power and perfect knowledge, reflecting the omnipotence and omniscience of Jesus.

- Purchased for God (Strong's G59): Emphasizes the redemptive price paid by Christ's sacrifice, highlighting the reconciliation achieved through His blood.

This passage underscores the central role of Jesus' sacrificial death in reconciling humanity to God, making it possible for people from every nation to become part of God's kingdom.

The Multitude Before the Throne

Key Verses: Revelation 7:9-17

The vision of the great multitude before the throne illustrates the fulfillment of reconciliation, with believers from all nations standing redeemed and united in worship.

- Revelation 7:9-10 (NIV): "After this I looked, and there before me was a great multitude that no one could count, from every nation, tribe, people and language, standing before the throne and before the Lamb. They were wearing white robes and were holding palm branches in their hands. And they cried out in a loud voice: 'Salvation belongs to our God, who sits on the throne, and to the Lamb.'"

Expository Insights:

- Great Multitude (Strong's G3793): Represents the inclusive and diverse nature of God's redeemed people, highlighting the global scope of Christ's reconciliation.

- White Robes (Strong's G4749): Symbolize purity and victory, reflecting the righteousness imparted by Christ through reconciliation.

- Palm Branches (Strong's G5404): Signify celebration and victory, pointing to the triumph of salvation and reconciliation.

Key Verses: Revelation 7:13-17

- Revelation 7:13-17 (NIV): "Then one of the elders asked me, 'These in white robes—who are they, and where did they come from?' I answered, 'Sir, you know.' And he said, 'These are they who have come out of the great tribulation; they have washed their robes and made them white in the blood of the Lamb. Therefore, they are before the throne of God and serve him day and night in his temple; and he who sits on the throne will shelter them with his presence. Never again will they hunger; never again will they thirst. The sun will not beat down on them,' nor any scorching heat. For the Lamb at the center of the throne will be their shepherd; he will lead them to springs of living water. And God will wipe away every tear from their eyes.'"

Expository Insights:

- Washed in the Blood of the Lamb (Strong's G4150 and G721): Indicates the cleansing and reconciling power of Jesus' sacrifice.

- Shelter Them with His Presence (Strong's G4637): Emphasizes the security and protection found in reconciliation with God.

- Lamb as Shepherd (Strong's G4165): Depicts Jesus' role in guiding and caring for the reconciled believers.

This vision highlights the transformative impact of reconciliation, resulting in a diverse and unified body of believers who find protection and nourishment in Christ.

The New Heaven and the New Earth

Key Verses: Revelation 21:1-5

The vision of the new heaven and new earth encapsulates the ultimate fulfillment of reconciliation, where God and humanity dwell together in perfect harmony.

- Revelation 21:1-5 (NIV): "Then I saw 'a new heaven and a new earth,' for the first heaven and the first earth had passed away, and there was no longer any sea. I saw the Holy

City, the new Jerusalem, coming down out of heaven from God, prepared as a bride beautifully dressed for her husband. And I heard a loud voice from the throne saying, 'Look! God's dwelling place is now among the people, and he will dwell with them. They will be his people, and God himself will be with them and be their God. He will wipe every tear from their eyes. There will be no more death or mourning or crying or pain, for the old order of things has passed away.' He who was seated on the throne said, 'I am making everything new!' Then he said, 'Write this down, for these words are trustworthy and true.'"

Expository Insights:

- New Heaven and New Earth (Strong's G2537 and G1093): Signify the complete renewal and restoration of creation, reflecting the ultimate reconciliation through Christ.

- New Jerusalem (Strong's G2419): Represents the redeemed community of God's people, united and reconciled in Christ.

- God's Dwelling Place (Strong's G4637): Emphasizes the intimate and eternal relationship between God and His reconciled people.

This vision offers a powerful picture of the ultimate reconciliation achieved through Christ, resulting in a renewed creation where God dwells with His people in perfect harmony.

The Eternal Reign of Christ

Key Verses: Revelation 22:1-5

The vision of the eternal reign of Christ highlights the final and complete reconciliation of all things, where believers enjoy eternal life and fellowship with God.

- Revelation 22:1-5 (NIV): "Then the angel showed me the river of the water of life, as clear as crystal, flowing from the throne of God and of the Lamb down the middle of the great street of the city. On each side of the river stood the tree of life, bearing twelve crops of fruit, yielding its fruit every month. And the leaves of the tree are for the healing of the nations. No longer will there be any curse. The throne of God and of the Lamb will be in the city, and his servants will serve him. They will see his face, and his name will be on their foreheads. There will be no more nights. They will not need the light of a lamp or the light of the sun, for the Lord God will give them light. And they will reign for ever and ever."

Expository Insights:

- River of the Water of Life (Strong's G5204): Symbolizes the eternal life and sustenance provided by Christ.

- Tree of Life (Strong's G3586 and G2222): Represents the fullness of life and healing available through reconciliation with God.

- Healing of the Nations (Strong's G2322 and G1484): Emphasizes the comprehensive and restorative nature of Christ's reconciliation.

- No Longer Any Curse (Strong's G2671): Indicates the complete removal of sin and its consequences, highlighting the perfect state of reconciliation.

This passage affirms the eternal and complete reconciliation achieved through Christ, where believers enjoy everlasting life and fellowship with God.

Practical Implications of Reconciliation Through Christ

1. Peace with God: Understanding reconciliation through Christ assures believers of peace with God, removing the barrier of sin and restoring a right relationship with Him.

2. Unity in Diversity: Embracing reconciliation fosters unity among believers from diverse backgrounds, as all are equally redeemed and reconciled in Christ.

3. Hope and Assurance: The promise of ultimate reconciliation provides believers with hope and assurance, even in the face of suffering and trials.

4. Transformative Living: Recognizing the transformative power of reconciliation encourages believers to live in a manner that reflects their new identity in Christ.

5. Eternal Perspective: Embracing the vision of ultimate reconciliation shifts believers' focus from temporal concerns to the eternal promises of God, inspiring them to live with purpose and anticipation of the renewed creation.

Conclusion

The Book of Revelation vividly portrays the theme of reconciliation through Christ through powerful imagery and declarations. From the depiction of the Lamb who was slain to the vision of the great multitude before the throne, and from the new heaven and new earth to the eternal reign of Christ, Revelation affirms the profound reconciliation achieved through Jesus' sacrificial death. As we reflect on these truths, we are encouraged to embrace the peace, unity, hope, and transformative power of reconciliation in our lives. Recognizing the significance of reconciliation through Christ transforms our understanding of our relationship with God and our place in His eternal kingdom, grounding us in His eternal purpose and love.

The fullness of God in Jesus

Key Verse: Colossians 1:19-20

Lesson: For God was pleased to have all His fullness dwell in Him, and through Him to reconcile to Himself all things, whether things on earth or things in heaven, by making peace through His blood, shed on the cross.

Fullness of God in Jesus: An Expository Study in the Book of Revelation

Introduction

The concept of the fullness of God dwelling in Jesus is a profound truth in Christian theology. It emphasizes the complete presence and essence of God in Christ, highlighting His divinity and supreme authority. The Book of Revelation vividly portrays this fullness through its rich imagery and declarations. This chapter will explore the theme of the fullness of God in Jesus as exhibited in Revelation, using an expository study method with references from Strong's Concordance.

Jesus, the Alpha and the Omega

Key Verses: Revelation 1:8, 21:6, 22:13

Revelation introduces Jesus as the Alpha and the Omega, underscoring His eternal nature and the fullness of His divinity.

- Revelation 1:8 (NIV): "I am the Alpha and the Omega," says the Lord God, "who is, and who was, and who is to come, the Almighty."

- Revelation 21:6 (NIV): "He said to me: 'It is done. I am the Alpha and the Omega, the Beginning and the End. To the thirsty I will give water without cost from the spring of the water of life.'"

- Revelation 22:13 (NIV): "I am the Alpha and the Omega, the First and the Last, the Beginning and the End."

Expository Insights:

- Alpha and Omega (Strong's G1 and G5598): Represent the first and last letters of the Greek alphabet, indicating Jesus' eternal existence and His encompassing presence in all things.

- The Almighty (Strong's G3841): Affirms Jesus' supreme power and authority, reflecting His divine nature.

These verses highlight the completeness and eternal nature of Jesus, emphasizing His role as the beginning and end of all things, which assures believers of His sovereign control and divine presence.

The Vision of the Glorified Christ

Key Verses: Revelation 1:12-18

John's vision of the glorified Christ provides a powerful image of Jesus' divine attributes and the fullness of God dwelling in Him.

- Revelation 1:12-18 (NIV): "I turned around to see the voice that was speaking to me. And when I turned I saw seven golden lampstands, and among the lampstands was someone like a son of man, dressed in a robe reaching down to his feet and with a golden sash around his chest. The hair on his head was white like wool, as white as snow, and his eyes were like blazing fire. His feet were like bronze glowing in a furnace, and his voice was like the sound of rushing waters. In his right hand he held seven stars, and coming out of his mouth was a sharp, double-edged sword. His face was like the sun shining in all its brilliance."

Expository Insights:

- Seven Golden Lampstands (Strong's G3087): Represent the seven churches, indicating Christ's presence among His people.

- Son of Man (Strong's G5207 and G444): A title emphasizing Jesus' humanity and divinity, rooted in Daniel 7:13-14.

- White Hair (Strong's G3022): Symbolizes purity, holiness, and eternal wisdom, reflecting the Ancient of Days (Daniel 7:9).

- Blazing Eyes (Strong's G3788): Denote His penetrating vision and omniscience.

- Glowing Feet (Strong's G5474): Represent judgment and strength.

- Voice Like Rushing Waters (Strong's G5456): Emphasizes the power and authority of His words.

- Double-edged Sword (Strong's G4501): Symbolizes the discerning and powerful nature of His word.

- Face Like the Sun (Strong's G2246): Reflects His divine glory and brilliance.

This vision underscores the divine attributes of Jesus, affirming that He embodies the fullness of God's presence and authority.

The Lamb Who Was Slain

Key Verses: Revelation 5:6-14

The depiction of Jesus as the Lamb who was slain highlights His redemptive role and the fullness of His divine authority and power.

- Revelation 5:6-7 (NIV): "Then I saw a Lamb, looking as if it had been slain, standing at the center of the throne, encircled by the four living creatures and the elders. The Lamb had seven horns and seven eyes, which are the seven spirits of God sent out into all the earth. He came and took the scroll from the right hand of him who sat on the throne."

Expository Insights:

- Lamb (Strong's G721): Represents Jesus' sacrificial role, emphasizing His redemptive work.

- Seven Horns and Seven Eyes (Strong's G2768 and G3788): Symbolize complete power and perfect knowledge, underscoring Jesus' omnipotence and omniscience.

- Seven Spirits of God (Strong's G4151): Indicate the fullness of the Holy Spirit, reflecting the divine nature of Jesus.

Key Verses: Revelation 5:12-13

- Revelation 5:12-13 (NIV): "In a loud voice they were saying: 'Worthy is the Lamb, who was slain, to receive power and wealth and wisdom and strength and honor and glory and praise!' Then I heard every creature in heaven and on earth and under the earth and on the sea, and all that is in them, saying: 'To him who sits on the throne and to the Lamb be praise and honor and glory and power, for ever and ever!'"

Expository Insights:

- Worthy (Strong's G514): Denotes deserving honor and reverence.

- Power, Wealth, Wisdom, Strength, Honor, Glory, and Praise (Strong's G1411, G4149, G4678, G2479, G5092, G1391, and G1868): Highlight the comprehensive nature of the attributes ascribed to Jesus, reflecting His complete divinity.

These passages affirm the fullness of divine attributes and authority in Jesus, encouraging believers to offer Him the highest praise and worship.

The New Heaven and the New Earth

Key Verses: Revelation 21:1-7

The vision of the new heaven and new earth underscores the fullness of God's presence in Jesus, who brings about the ultimate renewal of creation.

- Revelation 21:1-4 (NIV): "Then I saw 'a new heaven and a new earth,' for the first heaven and the first earth had passed away, and there was no longer any sea. I saw the Holy City, the new Jerusalem, coming down out of heaven from God, prepared as a bride beautifully dressed for her husband. And I heard a loud voice from the throne saying, 'Look! God's dwelling place is now among the people, and he will dwell with them. They will be his people, and God himself will be with them and be their God. He will wipe every tear from their eyes. There will be no more death or mourning or crying or pain, for the old order of things has passed away.'"

Expository Insights:

- New Heaven and New Earth (Strong's G2537 and G1093): Signify the complete renewal and restoration of creation by Jesus.

- New Jerusalem (Strong's G2419): Represents the redeemed community of God's people, created anew in Christ.

- God's Dwelling Place (Strong's G4637): Emphasizes the intimate and eternal relationship between God and His people.

This vision highlights the ultimate fulfillment of God's presence in Jesus, bringing about a renewed creation where God dwells with His people in perfect harmony.

The Eternal Reign of Christ

Key Verses: Revelation 22:1-5

The vision of the eternal reign of Christ illustrates the fullness of God's presence and authority in Jesus, who rules eternally over His redeemed people.

- Revelation 22:1-5 (NIV): "Then the angel showed me the river of the water of life, as clear as crystal, flowing from the throne of God and of the Lamb down the middle of the great street of the city. On each side of the river stood the tree of life, bearing twelve crops of fruit, yielding its fruit every month. And the leaves of the tree are for the healing of the nations. No longer will there be any curse. The throne of God and of the Lamb will be in the city, and his servants will serve him. They will see his face, and his name will be on their foreheads. There will be no more nights. They will not need the light of a lamp or the light of the sun, for the Lord God will give them light. And they will reign forever and ever."

Expository Insights:

- River of the Water of Life (Strong's G5204): Symbolizes the eternal life and sustenance provided by Christ.

- Tree of Life (Strong's G3586 and G2222): Represents the fullness of life and healing available through Jesus.

- Throne of God and of the Lamb (Strong's G2362 and G721): Emphasizes the unified and eternal reign of God and Jesus.

This passage affirms the eternal and complete reign of Christ, who embodies the fullness of God's presence and authority.

Practical Implications of the Fullness of God in Jesus

1. Complete Worship: Recognizing the fullness of God in Jesus calls believers to offer complete and wholehearted worship, acknowledging His divinity and supreme authority.

2. Assured Faith: Understanding that all the fullness of God dwells in Jesus provides believers with assurance and confidence in their faith, knowing they are united with the divine.

3. Transformative Living: Embracing the fullness of God in Jesus inspires believers to live transformed lives, reflecting His character and embodying His love and grace.

4. Eternal Perspective: The promise of the new heaven and new earth shifts believers' focus from temporal concerns to the eternal reality of God's kingdom, encouraging them to live with purpose and hope.

5. Unified Community: The vision of the new Jerusalem emphasizes the unity of the redeemed community, encouraging believers to foster unity and love within the church.

Conclusion

The Book of Revelation vividly portrays the fullness of God in Jesus through powerful imagery and declarations. From the depiction of Jesus as the Alpha and the Omega to the vision of the glorified Christ, and from the Lamb who was slain to the new heaven and new earth, Revelation affirms the complete presence and authority of God in Christ. As we reflect on these truths, we are encouraged to offer complete worship, live assured and transformed lives, maintain an eternal perspective, and foster unity within the community of believers. Recognizing the fullness of God in Jesus transforms our understanding of our faith and our relationship with Him, grounding us in His eternal purpose and love.

Reconciliation

Key Verse: Colossians 1:19-20

Lesson: For God was pleased to have all His fullness dwell in Him, and through Him to reconcile to Himself all things, whether things on earth or things in heaven, by making peace through His blood, shed on the cross.

Reconciliation: An Expository Study in the Book of Revelation

Introduction

The theme of reconciliation is central to the Christian faith, focusing on how Jesus' sacrificial death restores the broken relationship between God and humanity. The Book of Revelation, with its rich symbolism and profound declarations, vividly portrays this reconciliation and its ultimate fulfillment. This chapter will explore the theme of reconciliation as exhibited in Revelation, using an expository study method with references from Strong's Concordance.

The Lamb Who Was Slain

Key Verses: Revelation 5:6-10

The depiction of Jesus as the Lamb who was slain underscores His role in reconciliation and redemption.

- Revelation 5:6-10 (NIV): "Then I saw a Lamb, looking as if it had been slain, standing at the center of the throne, encircled by the four living creatures and the elders.

The Lamb had seven horns and seven eyes, which are the seven spirits of God sent out into all the earth. He went and took the scroll from the right hand of him who sat on the throne. And when he had taken it, the four living creatures and the twenty-four elders fell down before the Lamb. Each one had a harp and they were holding golden bowls full of incense, which are the prayers of God's people. And they sang a new song, saying: 'You are worthy to take the scroll and to open its seals, because you were slain, and with your blood you purchased for God persons from every tribe and language and people and nation. You have made them to be a kingdom and priests to serve our God, and they will reign on the earth.'"

Expository Insights:

- Lamb (Strong's G721): Represents Jesus' sacrificial role, emphasizing His redemptive work.

- Seven Horns and Seven Eyes (Strong's G2768 and G3788): Symbolize complete power and perfect knowledge, reflecting the omnipotence and omniscience of Jesus.

- Purchased for God (Strong's G59): Emphasizes the redemptive price paid by Christ's sacrifice, highlighting the reconciliation achieved through His blood.

This passage highlights the central role of Jesus' sacrificial death in reconciling humanity to God, making it possible for people from every nation to become part of God's kingdom.

The Multitude Before the Throne

Key Verses: Revelation 7:9-17

The vision of the great multitude before the throne illustrates the fulfillment of reconciliation, with believers from all nations standing redeemed and united in worship.

- Revelation 7:9-10 (NIV): "After this I looked, and there before me was a great multitude that no one could count, from every nation, tribe, people and language, standing before the throne and before the Lamb. They were wearing white robes and were holding palm branches in their hands. And they cried out in a loud voice: 'Salvation belongs to our God, who sits on the throne, and to the Lamb.'"

Expository Insights:

- Great Multitude (Strong's G3793): Represents the inclusive and diverse nature of God's redeemed people, highlighting the global scope of Christ's reconciliation.

- White Robes (Strong's G4749): Symbolize purity and victory, reflecting the righteousness imparted by Christ through reconciliation.

- Palm Branches (Strong's G5404): Signify celebration and victory, pointing to the triumph of salvation and reconciliation.

Key Verses: Revelation 7:13-17

- Revelation 7:13-17 (NIV): "Then one of the elders asked me, 'These in white robes—who are they, and where did they come from?' I answered, 'Sir, you know.' And he said, 'These are they who have come out of the great tribulation; they have washed their robes and made them white in the blood of the Lamb. Therefore, they are before the throne of God and serve him day and night in his temple; and he who sits on the throne will shelter them with his presence. Never again will they hunger; never again will they thirst. The sun will not beat down on them,' nor any scorching heat. For the Lamb at the center of the throne will be their shepherd; he will lead them to springs of living water. And God will wipe away every tear from their eyes.'"

Expository Insights:

- Washed in the Blood of the Lamb (Strong's G4150 and G721): Indicates the cleansing and reconciling power of Jesus' sacrifice.

- Shelter Them with His Presence (Strong's G4637): Emphasizes the security and protection found in reconciliation with God.

- Lamb as Shepherd (Strong's G4165): Depicts Jesus' role in guiding and caring for the reconciled believers.

This vision highlights the transformative impact of reconciliation, resulting in a diverse and unified body of believers who find protection and nourishment in Christ.

The New Heaven and the New Earth

Key Verses: Revelation 21:1-5

The vision of the new heaven and new earth encapsulates the ultimate fulfillment of reconciliation, where God and humanity dwell together in perfect harmony.

- Revelation 21:1-5 (NIV): "Then I saw 'a new heaven and a new earth,' for the first heaven and the first earth had passed away, and there was no longer any sea. I saw the Holy City, the new Jerusalem, coming down out of heaven from God, prepared as a bride beautifully dressed for her husband. And I heard a loud voice from the throne saying, 'Look! God's dwelling place is now among the people, and he will dwell with them. They will be his people, and God himself will be with them and be their God. He will wipe every tear from their eyes. There will be no more death or mourning or crying or pain, for the old order of things has passed away.' He who was seated on the throne said, 'I am making everything new!' Then he said, 'Write this down, for these words are trustworthy and true.'"

Expository Insights:

- New Heaven and New Earth (Strong's G2537 and G1093): Signify the complete renewal and restoration of creation, reflecting the ultimate reconciliation through Christ.

- New Jerusalem (Strong's G2419): Represents the redeemed community of God's people, united and reconciled in Christ.

- God's Dwelling Place (Strong's G4637): Emphasizes the intimate and eternal relationship between God and His reconciled people.

This vision offers a powerful picture of the ultimate reconciliation achieved through Christ, resulting in a renewed creation where God dwells with His people in perfect harmony.

The Eternal Reign of Christ

Key Verses: Revelation 22:1-5

The vision of the eternal reign of Christ highlights the final and complete reconciliation of all things, where believers enjoy eternal life and fellowship with God.

- Revelation 22:1-5 (NIV): "Then the angel showed me the river of the water of life, as clear as crystal, flowing from the throne of God and of the Lamb down the middle of the great street of the city. On each side of the river stood the tree of life, bearing twelve crops of fruit, yielding its fruit every month. And the leaves of the tree are for the healing of the nations. No longer will there be any curse. The throne of God and of the Lamb will be in the city, and his servants will serve him. They will see his face, and his name will be on their foreheads. There will be no more night. They will not need the light of a lamp or the light of the sun, for the Lord God will give them light. And they will reign for ever and ever."

Expository Insights:

- River of the Water of Life (Strong's G5204): Symbolizes the eternal life and sustenance provided by Christ.

- Tree of Life (Strong's G3586 and G2222): Represents the fullness of life and healing available through reconciliation with God.

- Healing of the Nations (Strong's G2322 and G1484): Emphasizes the comprehensive and restorative nature of Christ's reconciliation.

- No Longer Any Curse (Strong's G2671): Indicates the complete removal of sin and its consequences, highlighting the perfect state of reconciliation.

This passage affirms the eternal and complete reconciliation achieved through Christ, where believers enjoy everlasting life and fellowship with God.

Practical Implications of Reconciliation Through Christ

1. Peace with God: Understanding reconciliation through Christ assures believers of peace with God, removing the barrier of sin and restoring a right relationship with Him.

2. Unity in Diversity: Embracing reconciliation fosters unity among believers from diverse backgrounds, as all are equally redeemed and reconciled in Christ.

3. Hope and Assurance: The promise of ultimate reconciliation provides believers with hope and assurance, even in the face of suffering and trials.

4. Transformative Living: Recognizing the transformative power of reconciliation encourages believers to live in a manner that reflects their new identity in Christ.

5. Eternal Perspective: Embracing the vision of ultimate reconciliation shifts believers' focus from temporal concerns to the eternal promises of God, inspiring them to live with purpose and anticipation of the renewed creation.

Conclusion

The Book of Revelation vividly portrays the theme of reconciliation through Christ through powerful imagery and declarations. From the depiction of the Lamb who was slain to the vision of the great multitude before the throne, and from the new heaven and new earth to the eternal reign of Christ, Revelation affirms the profound reconciliation achieved through Jesus' sacrificial death. As we reflect on these truths, we are encouraged to embrace the peace, unity, hope, and transformative power of reconciliation in our lives. Recognizing the significance of reconciliation through Christ transforms our understanding of our relationship with God and our place in His eternal kingdom, grounding us in His eternal purpose and love.

Peace Through the Cross

Key Verse: Colossians 1:19-20

Lesson: For God was pleased to have all His fullness dwell in Him, and through Him to reconcile to Himself all things, whether things on earth or things in heaven, by making peace through His blood, shed on the cross.

Peace Through the Cross: An Expository Study in the Book of Revelation

Introduction

The peace brought by Jesus' sacrificial death on the cross is a central theme in Christian theology. This peace not only reconciles individuals to God but also extends to the entire creation, promising ultimate restoration and harmony. The Book of Revelation powerfully illustrates the impact of this peace through its vivid imagery and profound declarations. This chapter will explore the theme of peace through the cross as exhibited in Revelation, using an expository study method with references from Strong's Concordance.

The Lamb Who Was Slain

Key Verses: Revelation 5:6-10

The depiction of Jesus as the Lamb who was slain emphasizes the peace and reconciliation achieved through His sacrificial death.

- Revelation 5:6-10 (NIV): "Then I saw a Lamb, looking as if it had been slain, standing at the center of the throne, encircled by the four living creatures and the elders. The Lamb had seven horns and seven eyes, which are the seven spirits of God sent out into all the earth. He went and took the scroll from the right hand of him who sat on the throne. And when he had taken it, the four living creatures and the twenty-four elders fell down before the Lamb. Each one had a harp and they were holding golden bowls full of incense, which are the prayers of God's people. And they sang a new song, saying: 'You are worthy to take the scroll and to open its seals, because you were slain, and with your blood you purchased for God persons from every tribe and language and people and nation. You have made them to be a kingdom and priests to serve our God, and they will reign on the earth.'"

Expository Insights:

- Lamb (Strong's G721): Represents Jesus' sacrificial role, emphasizing His redemptive work.

- Seven Horns and Seven Eyes (Strong's G2768 and G3788): Symbolize complete power and perfect knowledge, reflecting the omnipotence and omniscience of Jesus.

- Purchased for God (Strong's G59): Emphasizes the redemptive price paid by Christ's sacrifice, highlighting the peace and reconciliation achieved through His blood.

This passage underscores the central role of Jesus' sacrificial death in bringing peace, making it possible for people from every nation to be reconciled to God and to each other.

The Multitude Before the Throne

Key Verses: Revelation 7:9-17

The vision of the great multitude before the throne illustrates the fulfillment of peace, with believers from all nations standing redeemed and united in worship.

- Revelation 7:9-10 (NIV): "After this I looked, and there before me was a great multitude that no one could count, from every nation, tribe, people and language, standing before the throne and before the Lamb. They were wearing white robes and were holding palm branches in their hands. And they cried out in a loud voice: 'Salvation belongs to our God, who sits on the throne, and to the Lamb.'"

Expository Insights:

- Great Multitude (Strong's G3793): Represents the inclusive and diverse nature of God's redeemed people, highlighting the global scope of Christ's peace.

- White Robes (Strong's G4749): Symbolize purity and victory, reflecting the righteousness imparted by Christ through His sacrifice.

- Palm Branches (Strong's G5404): Signify celebration and victory, pointing to the triumph of peace and reconciliation.

Key Verses: Revelation 7:13-17

- Revelation 7:13-17 (NIV): "Then one of the elders asked me, 'These in white robes—who are they, and where did they come from?' I answered, 'Sir, you know.' And he said, 'These are they who have come out of the great tribulation; they have washed their robes and made them white in the blood of the Lamb. Therefore, they are before the throne of God and serve him day and night in his temple; and he who sits on the throne will shelter them with his presence. Never again will they hunger; never again will they thirst. The sun will not beat down on them,' nor any scorching heat. For the Lamb at the center of the throne will be their shepherd; he will lead them to springs of living water. And God will wipe away every tear from their eyes.'"

Expository Insights:

- Washed in the Blood of the Lamb (Strong's G4150 and G721): Indicates the cleansing and peace brought by Jesus' sacrifice.

- Shelter Them with His Presence (Strong's G4637): Emphasizes the security and peace found in reconciliation with God.

- Lamb as Shepherd (Strong's G4165): Depicts Jesus' role in guiding and caring for the reconciled believers.

This vision highlights the transformative impact of Jesus' sacrificial death, resulting in a diverse and unified body of believers who find peace and security in Christ.

The New Heaven and the New Earth

Key Verses: Revelation 21:1-5

The vision of the new heaven and new earth encapsulates the ultimate fulfillment of peace through Jesus' sacrifice, where God and humanity dwell together in perfect harmony.

- Revelation 21:1-5 (NIV): "Then I saw 'a new heaven and a new earth,' for the first heaven and the first earth had passed away, and there was no longer any sea. I saw the Holy City, the new Jerusalem, coming down out of heaven from God, prepared as a bride beautifully dressed for her husband. And I heard a loud voice from the throne saying, 'Look! God's dwelling place is now among the people, and he will dwell with them. They will be his people, and God himself will be with them and be their God. He will wipe every tear from their eyes. There will be no more death or mourning or crying or pain, for the old order of things has passed away.' He who was seated on the throne said, 'I am making everything new!' Then he said, 'Write this down, for these words are trustworthy and true.'"

Expository Insights:

- New Heaven and New Earth (Strong's G2537 and G1093): Signify the complete renewal and restoration of creation, reflecting the ultimate peace through Christ.

- New Jerusalem (Strong's G2419): Represents the redeemed community of God's people, united in peace through Christ.

- God's Dwelling Place (Strong's G4637): Emphasizes the intimate and eternal relationship between God and His reconciled people.

This vision offers a powerful picture of the ultimate peace achieved through Jesus, resulting in a renewed creation where God dwells with His people in perfect harmony.

The Eternal Reign of Christ

Key Verses: Revelation 22:1-5

The vision of the eternal reign of Christ highlights the final and complete peace brought by Jesus' sacrificial death, where believers enjoy eternal life and fellowship with God.

- Revelation 22:1-5 (NIV): "Then the angel showed me the river of the water of life, as clear as crystal, flowing from the throne of God and of the Lamb down the middle of the great street of the city. On each side of the river stood the tree of life, bearing twelve crops of fruit, yielding its fruit every month. And the leaves of the tree are for the healing of the nations. No longer will there be any curse. The throne of God and of the Lamb will be in the city, and his servants will serve him. They will see his face, and his name will be on their foreheads. There will be no more night. They will not need the light of a lamp or the light of the sun, for the Lord God will give them light. And they will reign for ever and ever."

Expository Insights:

- River of the Water of Life (Strong's G5204): Symbolizes the eternal life and sustenance provided by Christ.

- Tree of Life (Strong's G3586 and G2222): Represents the fullness of life and healing available through reconciliation with God.

- Healing of the Nations (Strong's G2322 and G1484): Emphasizes the comprehensive and restorative nature of Christ's peace.

- No Longer Any Curse (Strong's G2671): Indicates the complete removal of sin and its consequences, highlighting the perfect state of peace.

This passage affirms the eternal and complete peace achieved through Jesus, where believers enjoy everlasting life and fellowship with God.

Practical Implications of Peace Through the Cross

1. Inner Peace: Understanding the peace brought by Jesus' sacrifice provides believers with inner peace, knowing they are reconciled to God and free from the burden of sin.

2. Unity and Reconciliation: Embracing the peace of Christ fosters unity among believers, encouraging reconciliation and harmonious relationships within the body of Christ.

3. Hope and Assurance: The promise of ultimate peace provides believers with hope and assurance, even in the face of suffering and trials.

4. Transformative Living: Recognizing the transformative power of Jesus' sacrifice encourages believers to live in a manner that reflects the peace and reconciliation they have received.

5. Eternal Perspective: Embracing the vision of

ultimate peace shifts believers' focus from temporal concerns to the eternal promises of God, inspiring them to live with purpose and anticipation of the renewed creation.

Conclusion

The Book of Revelation vividly portrays the theme of peace through the cross through powerful imagery and declarations. From the depiction of the Lamb who was slain to the vision of the great multitude before the throne, and from the new heaven and new earth to the eternal reign of Christ, Revelation affirms the profound peace achieved through Jesus' sacrificial death. As we reflect on these truths, we are encouraged to embrace the inner peace, unity, hope, and transformative power of Jesus' sacrifice in our lives. Recognizing the significance of peace through the cross transforms our understanding of our relationship with God and our place in His eternal kingdom, grounding us in His eternal purpose and love.

CHAPTER 06

THE MYSTERY OF CHRIST IN YOU

Key Verse: Colossians 1:26-27

Lesson: The mystery that has been kept hidden for ages and generations, but is now disclosed to the Lord's people. To them God has chosen to make known among the Gentiles the glorious riches of this mystery, which is Christ in you, the hope of glory.

The Mystery of Christ in You: An Expository Study in the Book of Revelation

Introduction

The mystery of "Christ in you, the hope of glory" is a profound truth in Christian theology. It speaks to the indwelling presence of Christ in believers, offering the hope of eternal glory. The Book of Revelation, with its rich symbolism and profound declarations, provides deep insights into this mystery. This chapter will explore the theme of the mystery of Christ in you as exhibited in Revelation, using an expository study method with references from Strong's Concordance.

Christ Among the Lampstands

Key Verses: Revelation 1:12-20

John's vision of Christ among the seven golden lampstands offers a powerful image of His presence within the church, symbolizing His indwelling presence in believers.

- Revelation 1:12-13 (NIV): "I turned around to see the voice that was speaking to me. And when I turned I saw seven golden lampstands, and among the lampstands was someone like a son of man, dressed in a robe reaching down to his feet and with a golden sash around his chest."

Expository Insights:

- Seven Golden Lampstands (Strong's G3087): Represent the seven churches, indicating Christ's presence among His people.

- Son of Man (Strong's G5207 and G444): A title emphasizing Jesus' humanity and divinity, rooted in Daniel 7:13-14.

Key Verses: Revelation 1:17-18

- Revelation 1:17-18 (NIV): "When I saw him, I fell at his feet as though dead. Then he placed his right hand on me and said: 'Do not be afraid. I am the First and the Last. I am the Living One; I was dead, and now look, I am alive for ever and ever! And I hold the keys of death and Hades.'"

Expository Insights:

- First and the Last (Strong's G4413 and G2078): Indicate Jesus' eternal nature and authority over all time.

- Living One (Strong's G2198): Emphasizes His resurrection and eternal life.

- Keys of Death and Hades (Strong's G2807, G2288, and G86): Symbolize His authority over life, death, and the afterlife.

This vision underscores Christ's supreme authority and His active presence within the church, symbolizing the mystery of Christ dwelling within believers.

The Overcomers Promised a Dwelling with Christ

Key Verses: Revelation 3:20-21

Jesus' message to the church in Laodicea highlights the intimate fellowship and indwelling presence He promises to those who overcome.

- Revelation 3:20-21 (NIV): "Here I am! I stand at the door and knock. If anyone hears my voice and opens the door, I will come in and eat with that person, and they with me. To the one who is victorious, I will give the right to sit with me on my throne, just as I was victorious and sat down with my Father on his throne."

Expository Insights:

- Stand at the Door and Knock (Strong's G2476 and G2925): Represents Jesus' invitation to intimate fellowship and presence within believers.

- Eat with That Person (Strong's G1172): Symbolizes intimate fellowship and communion.

- Sit with Me on My Throne (Strong's G2521 and G2362): Indicates the honor and authority shared with those who are united with Christ.

This promise emphasizes the indwelling presence of Christ in believers, offering them intimate fellowship and the hope of sharing in His eternal reign.

The New Jerusalem: God Dwelling with His People

Key Verses: Revelation 21:1-4

The vision of the new Jerusalem depicts the ultimate fulfillment of the mystery of Christ in believers, where God dwells with His people in perfect harmony.

- Revelation 21:1-4 (NIV): "Then I saw 'a new heaven and a new earth,' for the first heaven and the first earth had passed away, and there was no longer any sea. I saw the Holy

City, the new Jerusalem, coming down out of heaven from God, prepared as a bride beautifully dressed for her husband. And I heard a loud voice from the throne saying, 'Look! God's dwelling place is now among the people, and he will dwell with them. They will be his people, and God himself will be with them and be their God. He will wipe every tear from their eyes. There will be no more death or mourning or crying or pain, for the old order of things has passed away.'"

Expository Insights:

- New Heaven and New Earth (Strong's G2537 and G1093): Signify the complete renewal and restoration of creation.

- New Jerusalem (Strong's G2419): Represents the redeemed community of God's people, united in Christ.

- God's Dwelling Place (Strong's G4637): Emphasizes the intimate and eternal relationship between God and His people.

This vision highlights the ultimate fulfillment of Christ's indwelling presence, where believers experience perfect union and fellowship with God.

The River of the Water of Life

Key Verses: Revelation 22:1-5

The vision of the river of the water of life flowing from the throne of God and of the Lamb symbolizes the life-giving presence of Christ in believers, offering eternal nourishment and healing.

- Revelation 22:1-5 (NIV): "Then the angel showed me the river of the water of life, as clear as crystal, flowing from the throne of God and of the Lamb down the middle of the great street of the city. On each side of the river stood the tree of life, bearing twelve crops of fruit, yielding its fruit every month. And the leaves of the tree are for the healing of the nations. No longer will there be any curse. The throne of God and of the Lamb will be in the city, and his servants will serve him. They will see his face, and his name will be on their foreheads. There will be no more night. They will not need the light of a lamp or the light of the sun, for the Lord God will give them light. And they will reign for ever and ever."

Expository Insights:

- River of the Water of Life (Strong's G5204): Symbolizes the life-giving presence of Christ.

- Tree of Life (Strong's G3586 and G2222): Represents the fullness of life and healing available through Christ.

- Throne of God and of the Lamb (Strong's G2362 and G721): Emphasizes the unified and eternal reign of God and Jesus.

This passage affirms the eternal and life-giving presence of Christ in believers, offering them nourishment, healing, and eternal fellowship with God.

Practical Implications of the Mystery of Christ in You

1. Intimate Fellowship: Recognizing the indwelling presence of Christ encourages believers to cultivate intimate fellowship with Him, experiencing His life-giving presence daily.

2. Hope of Glory: Understanding that Christ in us is the hope of glory provides believers with assurance and confidence in their future with God.

3. Transformative Living: Embracing the mystery of Christ in us inspires believers to live transformed lives, reflecting His character and embodying His love and grace.

4. Unity with God: The promise of God dwelling with His people emphasizes the intimate and eternal relationship believers have with God, encouraging them to live in harmony with Him and with one another.

5. Eternal Perspective: Embracing the vision of the new Jerusalem and the river of the water of life shifts believers' focus from temporal concerns to the eternal reality of God's kingdom, inspiring them to live with purpose and anticipation of the renewed creation.

Conclusion

The Book of Revelation vividly portrays the mystery of Christ in believers through powerful imagery and declarations. From the vision of Christ among the lampstands to the promise of intimate fellowship with Him, and from the new Jerusalem to the river of the water of life, Revelation affirms the profound truth of Christ's indwelling presence. As we reflect on these truths, we are encouraged to embrace the intimate fellowship, hope, transformative power, and eternal perspective offered by the mystery of Christ in us. Recognizing the significance of this mystery transforms our understanding of our relationship with God and our place in His eternal kingdom, grounding us in His eternal purpose and love.

Revealed Mystery

Key Verse: Colossians 1:26-27

Lesson: The mystery that has been kept hidden for ages and generations, but is now disclosed to the Lord's people. To them God has chosen to make known among the Gentiles the glorious riches of this mystery, which is Christ in you, the hope of glory.

Revealed Mystery: An Expository Study in the Book of Revelation

Introduction

The revelation of God's mystery in Jesus is a profound truth that brings together both Jews and Gentiles into one unified body. This mystery, which was hidden for ages, is now disclosed through Christ, providing hope and glory for all believers. The Book of Revelation, with its rich imagery and profound declarations, provides deep insights into this revealed mystery. This chapter will explore the theme of the revealed mystery as exhibited in Revelation, using an expository study method with references from Strong's Concordance.

The Lamb Who Was Slain: Revealing the Mystery

Key Verses: Revelation 5:6-10

The depiction of Jesus as the Lamb who was slain reveals the central role of His sacrificial death in God's redemptive plan for both Jews and Gentiles.

- Revelation 5:6-10 (NIV): "Then I saw a Lamb, looking as if it had been slain, standing at the center of the throne, encircled by the four living creatures and the elders. The Lamb had seven horns and seven eyes, which are the seven spirits of God sent out into all the earth. He went and took the scroll from the right hand of him who sat on the throne. And when he had taken it, the four living creatures and the twenty-four elders fell down before the Lamb. Each one had a harp and they were holding golden bowls full of incense, which are the prayers of God's people. And they sang a new song, saying: 'You are worthy to take the scroll and to open its seals, because you were slain, and with your blood you purchased for God persons from every tribe and language and people and nation. You have made them to be a kingdom and priests to serve our God, and they will reign on the earth.'"

Expository Insights:

- Lamb (Strong's G721): Represents Jesus' sacrificial role, emphasizing His redemptive work.

- Seven Horns and Seven Eyes (Strong's G2768 and G3788): Symbolize complete power and perfect knowledge, reflecting the omnipotence and omniscience of Jesus.

- Purchased for God (Strong's G59): Emphasizes the redemptive price paid by Christ's sacrifice, highlighting the reconciliation achieved through His blood for people from every nation.

This passage highlights the central role of Jesus' sacrificial death in uniting both Jews and Gentiles into one redeemed community.

The Great Multitude Before the Throne

Key Verses: Revelation 7:9-17

The vision of the great multitude before the throne reveals the inclusive nature of God's redemptive plan, bringing together believers from all nations.

- Revelation 7:9-10 (NIV): "After this I looked, and there before me was a great multitude that no one could count, from every nation, tribe, people and language, standing before the throne and before the Lamb. They were wearing white robes and were holding palm branches in their hands. And they cried out in a loud voice: 'Salvation belongs to our God, who sits on the throne, and to the Lamb.'"

Expository Insights:

- Great Multitude (Strong's G3793): Represents the inclusive and diverse nature of God's redeemed people, highlighting the global scope of Christ's reconciliation.

- White Robes (Strong's G4749): Symbolize purity and victory, reflecting the righteousness imparted by Christ through His sacrifice.

- Palm Branches (Strong's G5404): Signify celebration and victory, pointing to the triumph of salvation and reconciliation.

Key Verses: Revelation 7:13-17

- Revelation 7:13-17 (NIV): "Then one of the elders asked me, 'These in white robes—who are they, and where did they come from?' I answered, 'Sir, you know.' And he said, 'These are they who have come out of the great tribulation; they have washed their robes and made them white in the blood of the Lamb. Therefore, they are before the throne of

God and serve him day and night in his temple; and he who sits on the throne will shelter them with his presence. Never again will they hunger; never again will they thirst. The sun will not beat down on them,' nor any scorching heat. For the Lamb at the center of the throne will be their shepherd; he will lead them to springs of living water. And God will wipe away every tear from their eyes.'"

Expository Insights:

- Washed in the Blood of the Lamb (Strong's G4150 and G721): Indicates the cleansing and reconciling power of Jesus' sacrifice.

- Shelter Them with His Presence (Strong's G4637): Emphasizes the security and protection found in reconciliation with God.

- Lamb as Shepherd (Strong's G4165): Depicts Jesus' role in guiding and caring for the reconciled believers.

This vision highlights the fulfillment of God's mystery, bringing together a diverse and unified body of believers who find protection and nourishment in Christ.

The New Jerusalem: A Unified Community

Key Verses: Revelation 21:1-5

The vision of the new Jerusalem reveals the ultimate fulfillment of God's mystery, where Jews and Gentiles dwell together in perfect harmony with God.

- Revelation 21:1-5 (NIV): "Then I saw 'a new heaven and a new earth,' for the first heaven and the first earth had passed away, and there was no longer any sea. I saw the Holy City, the new Jerusalem, coming down out of heaven from God, prepared as a bride beautifully dressed for her husband. And I heard a loud voice from the throne saying, 'Look! God's dwelling place is now among the people, and he will dwell with them. They will be his people, and God himself will be with them and be their God. He will wipe every tear from their eyes. There will be no more death or mourning or crying or pain, for the old order of things has passed away.'"

Expository Insights:

- New Heaven and New Earth (Strong's G2537 and G1093): Signify the complete renewal and restoration of creation, reflecting the ultimate reconciliation through Christ.

- New Jerusalem (Strong's G2419): Represents the redeemed community of God's people, united and reconciled in Christ.

- God's Dwelling Place (Strong's G4637): Emphasizes the intimate and eternal relationship between God and His reconciled people.

This vision offers a powerful picture of the ultimate fulfillment of God's mystery, where Jews and Gentiles are united in Christ, dwelling with God in perfect harmony.

The Eternal Reign of Christ

Key Verses: Revelation 22:1-5

The vision of the eternal reign of Christ highlights the complete and eternal nature of God's mystery revealed in Jesus, where believers enjoy eternal life and fellowship with God.

- Revelation 22:1-5 (NIV): "Then the angel showed me the river of the water of life, as clear as crystal, flowing from the throne of God and of the Lamb down the middle of the great street of the city. On each side of the river stood the tree of life, bearing twelve crops of fruit, yielding its fruit every month. And the leaves of the tree are for the healing of the nations. No longer will there be any curse. The throne of God and of the Lamb will be in the city, and his servants will serve him. They will see his face, and his name will be on their foreheads. There will be no more night. They will not need the light of a lamp or the light of the sun, for the Lord God will give them light. And they will reign for ever and ever."

Expository Insights:

- River of the Water of Life (Strong's G5204): Symbolizes the eternal life and sustenance provided by Christ.

- Tree of Life (Strong's G3586 and G2222): Represents the fullness of life and healing available through reconciliation with God.

- Healing of the Nations (Strong's G2322 and G1484): Emphasizes the comprehensive and restorative nature of Christ's reconciliation.

- No Longer Any Curse (Strong's G2671): Indicates the complete removal of sin and its consequences, highlighting the perfect state of reconciliation.

This passage affirms the eternal and complete fulfillment of God's mystery revealed in Jesus, where believers from all nations enjoy everlasting life and fellowship with God.

Practical Implications of the Revealed Mystery

1. Unified Community: Recognizing the revealed mystery of God in Jesus encourages believers to embrace unity within the body of Christ, transcending ethnic and cultural boundaries.

2. Inclusive Gospel: Understanding that God's mystery is revealed to both Jews and Gentiles motivates believers to share the gospel inclusively, reaching out to all people.

3. Hope and Assurance: The promise of ultimate reconciliation provides believers with hope and assurance, even in the face of suffering and trials.

4. Transformative Living: Embracing the revealed mystery inspires believers to live transformed lives, reflecting the unity and reconciliation achieved through Christ.

5. Eternal Perspective: The vision of the new Jerusalem and the eternal reign of Christ shifts believers' focus from temporal concerns to the eternal reality of God's kingdom, inspiring them to live with purpose and anticipation of the renewed creation.

Conclusion

The Book of Revelation vividly portrays the theme of the revealed mystery through powerful imagery and declarations. From the depiction of the Lamb who was slain to the vision of the great multitude before the throne, and from the new Jerusalem to the eternal reign of Christ, Revelation affirms the profound truth of God's mystery revealed in Jesus. As we reflect on these truths, we are encouraged to embrace the unity, hope, transformative power, and eternal perspective offered by the revealed mystery of Christ. Recognizing the significance of this mystery transforms our understanding of our relationship with God and our place in His eternal kingdom, grounding us in His eternal purpose and love.

Christ in You

Key Verse: Colossians 1:26-27

Lesson: The mystery that has been kept hidden for ages and generations, but is now disclosed to the Lord's people. To them God has chosen to make known among the Gentiles the glorious riches of this mystery, which is Christ in you, the hope of glory.

Christ in You: An Expository Study in the Book of Revelation

Introduction

The profound reality of Christ dwelling within believers is a cornerstone of Christian faith. This indwelling presence of Christ provides believers with hope, assurance, and transformative power. The Book of Revelation, with its rich symbolism and powerful imagery, offers deep insights into the reality of Christ in believers. This chapter will explore the theme of "Christ in you" as exhibited in Revelation, using an expository study method with references from Strong's Concordance.

The Presence of Christ Among the Churches

Key Verses: Revelation 1:12-20

John's vision of Christ among the seven golden lampstands symbolizes His presence within the church, highlighting His indwelling presence in believers.

- Revelation 1:12-13 (NIV): "I turned around to see the voice that was speaking to me. And when I turned I saw seven golden lampstands, and among the lampstands was someone like a son of man, dressed in a robe reaching down to his feet and with a golden sash around his chest."

Expository Insights:

- Seven Golden Lampstands (Strong's G3087): Represent the seven churches, indicating Christ's presence among His people.

- Son of Man (Strong's G5207 and G444): A title emphasizing Jesus' humanity and divinity, rooted in Daniel 7:13-14.

Key Verses: Revelation 1:17-18

- Revelation 1:17-18 (NIV): "When I saw him, I fell at his feet as though dead. Then he placed his right hand on me and said: 'Do not be afraid. I am the First and the Last. I am the Living One; I was dead, and now look, I am alive for ever and ever! And I hold the keys of death and Hades.'"

Expository Insights:

- First and the Last (Strong's G4413 and G2078): Indicate Jesus' eternal nature and authority over all time.

- Living One (Strong's G2198): Emphasizes His resurrection and eternal life.

- Keys of Death and Hades (Strong's G2807, G2288, and G86): Symbolize His authority over life, death, and the afterlife.

This vision underscores Christ's supreme authority and His active presence within the church, symbolizing the mystery of Christ dwelling within believers.

The Promise to Overcomers

Key Verses: Revelation 3:20-21

Jesus' message to the church in Laodicea highlights the intimate fellowship and indwelling presence He promises to those who overcome.

- Revelation 3:20-21 (NIV): "Here I am! I stand at the door and knock. If anyone hears my voice and opens the door, I will come in and eat with that person, and they with me. To the one who is victorious, I will give the right to sit with me on my throne, just as I was victorious and sat down with my Father on his throne."

Expository Insights:

- Stand at the Door and Knock (Strong's G2476 and G2925): Represents Jesus' invitation to intimate fellowship and presence within believers.

- Eat with That Person (Strong's G1172): Symbolizes intimate fellowship and communion.

- Sit with Me on My Throne (Strong's G2521 and G2362): Indicates the honor and authority shared with those who are united with Christ.

This promise emphasizes the indwelling presence of Christ in believers, offering them intimate fellowship and the hope of sharing in His eternal reign.

The New Jerusalem: God Dwelling with His People

Key Verses: Revelation 21:1-4

The vision of the new Jerusalem depicts the ultimate fulfillment of the mystery of Christ in believers, where God dwells with His people in perfect harmony.

- Revelation 21:1-4 (NIV): "Then I saw 'a new heaven and a new earth,' for the first heaven and the first earth had passed away, and there was no longer any sea. I saw the Holy City, the new Jerusalem, coming down out of heaven from God, prepared as a bride beautifully dressed for her husband. And I heard a loud voice from the throne saying, 'Look! God's dwelling place is now among the people, and he will dwell with them. They will be his people, and God himself will be with them and be their God. He will wipe every tear from their eyes. There will be no more death or mourning or crying or pain, for the old order of things has passed away.'"

Expository Insights:

- New Heaven and New Earth (Strong's G2537 and G1093): Signify the complete renewal and restoration of creation.

- New Jerusalem (Strong's G2419): Represents the redeemed community of God's people, united in Christ.

- God's Dwelling Place (Strong's G4637): Emphasizes the intimate and eternal relationship between God and His people.

This vision highlights the ultimate fulfillment of Christ's indwelling presence, where believers experience perfect union and fellowship with God.

The River of the Water of Life

Key Verses: Revelation 22:1-5

The vision of the river of the water of life flowing from the throne of God and of the Lamb symbolizes the life-giving presence of Christ in believers, offering eternal nourishment and healing.

Revelation 22:1-5 (NIV): "Then the angel showed me the river of the water of life, as clear as crystal, flowing from the throne of God and of the Lamb down the middle of the great street of the city. On each side of the river stood the tree of life, bearing twelve crops of fruit, yielding its fruit every month. And the leaves of the tree are for the healing of the nations. No longer will there be any curse. The throne of God and of the Lamb will be in the city, and his servants will serve him. They will see his face, and his name will be on their foreheads. There will be no more night. They will not need the light of a lamp or the light of the sun, for the Lord God will give them light. And they will reign for ever and ever."

Expository Insights:

- River of the Water of Life (Strong's G5204): Symbolizes the eternal life and sustenance provided by Christ.

- Tree of Life (Strong's G3586 and G2222): Represents the fullness of life and healing available through Christ.

- Throne of God and of the Lamb (Strong's G2362 and G721): Emphasizes the unified and eternal reign of God and Jesus.

This passage affirms the eternal and life-giving presence of Christ in believers, offering them nourishment, healing, and eternal fellowship with God.

Practical Implications of Christ in You

1. Intimate Fellowship: Recognizing the indwelling presence of Christ encourages believers to cultivate intimate fellowship with Him, experiencing His life-giving presence daily.

2. Hope of Glory: Understanding that Christ in us is the hope of glory provides believers with assurance and confidence in their future with God.

3. Transformative Living: Embracing the mystery of Christ in us inspires believers to live transformed lives, reflecting His character and embodying His love and grace.

4. Unity with God: The promise of God dwelling with His people emphasizes the intimate and eternal relationship believers have with God, encouraging them to live in harmony with Him and with one another.

5. Eternal Perspective: Embracing the vision of the new Jerusalem and the river of the water of life shifts believers' focus from temporal concerns to the eternal reality of God's kingdom, inspiring them to live with purpose and anticipation of the renewed creation.

Conclusion

The Book of Revelation vividly portrays the reality of Christ in believers through powerful imagery and declarations. From the vision of Christ among the lampstands to the promise of intimate fellowship with Him, and from the new Jerusalem to the river of the water of life, Revelation affirms the profound truth of Christ's indwelling presence. As we reflect on these truths, we are encouraged to embrace the intimate fellowship, hope, transformative power, and eternal perspective offered by the mystery of Christ in us. Recognizing the significance of this mystery transforms our understanding of our relationship with God and our place in

His eternal kingdom, grounding us in His eternal purpose and love.

Hope of Glory

Key Verse: Colossians 1:26-27

Lesson: The mystery that has been kept hidden for ages and generations, but is now disclosed to the Lord's people. To them God has chosen to make known among the Gentiles the glorious riches of this mystery, which is Christ in you, the hope of glory.

Hope of Glory: An Expository Study in the Book of Revelation

Introduction

The "hope of glory" encapsulates the future hope and glory that believers anticipate through their union with Christ. This hope is not just a distant dream but a profound reality that shapes the lives of Christians today. The Book of Revelation, with its vivid imagery and profound declarations, provides a rich tapestry of the future glory that awaits believers. This chapter will explore the theme of the "hope of glory" as exhibited in Revelation, using an expository study method with references from Strong's Concordance.

The Vision of the Glorified Christ

Key Verses: Revelation 1:12-18

John's vision of the glorified Christ sets the stage for understanding the future hope and glory believers share in through their union with Him.

- Revelation 1:12-18 (NIV): "I turned around to see the voice that was speaking to me. And when I turned I saw seven golden lampstands, and among the lampstands was someone like a son of man, dressed in a robe reaching down to his feet and with a golden sash around his chest. The hair on his head was white like wool, as white as snow, and his eyes were like blazing fire. His feet were like bronze glowing in a furnace, and his voice was like the sound of rushing waters. In his right hand he held seven stars, and coming out of his mouth was a sharp, double-edged sword. His face was like the sun shining in all its brilliance."

Expository Insights:

- Seven Golden Lampstands (Strong's G3087): Represent the seven churches, indicating Christ's presence among His people.

- Son of Man (Strong's G5207 and G444): A title emphasizing Jesus' humanity and divinity, rooted in Daniel 7:13-14.

- White Hair (Strong's G3022): Symbolizes purity, holiness, and eternal wisdom.

- Blazing Eyes (Strong's G3788): Denote His penetrating vision and omniscience.

- Glowing Feet (Strong's G5474): Represent judgment and strength.

- Voice Like Rushing Waters (Strong's G5456): Emphasizes the power and authority of His words.

- Double-edged Sword (Strong's G4501): Symbolizes the discerning and powerful nature of His word.

- Face Like the Sun (Strong's G2246): Reflects His divine glory and brilliance.

This vision underscores the future hope and glory that believers will share in through their union with the glorified Christ.

The Multitude Before the Throne

Key Verses: Revelation 7:9-17

The vision of the great multitude before the throne illustrates the ultimate fulfillment of the hope of glory, with believers from all nations standing redeemed and united in worship.

- Revelation 7:9-10 (NIV): "After this I looked, and there before me was a great multitude that no one could count, from every nation, tribe, people and language, standing before the throne and before the Lamb. They were wearing white robes and were holding palm branches in their hands.

And they cried out in a loud voice: 'Salvation belongs to our God, who sits on the throne, and to the Lamb.'"

Expository Insights:

- Great Multitude (Strong's G3793): Represents the inclusive and diverse nature of God's redeemed people, highlighting the global scope of Christ's reconciliation.

- White Robes (Strong's G4749): Symbolize purity and victory, reflecting the righteousness imparted by Christ through reconciliation.

- Palm Branches (Strong's G5404): Signify celebration and victory, pointing to the triumph of salvation and reconciliation.

Key Verses: Revelation 7:13-17

- Revelation 7:13-17 (NIV): "Then one of the elders asked me, 'These in white robes—who are they, and where did they come from?' I answered, 'Sir, you know.' And he said, 'These are they who have come out of the great tribulation; they have washed their robes and made them white in the blood of the Lamb. Therefore, they are before the throne of God and serve him day and night in his temple; and he who sits on the throne will shelter them with his presence. Never again will they hunger; never again will they thirst. The sun will not beat down on them,' nor any scorching heat. For the Lamb at the center of the throne will be their shepherd; he will lead them to springs of living water. And God will wipe away every tear from their eyes.'"

Expository Insights:

- Washed in the Blood of the Lamb (Strong's G4150 and G721): Indicates the cleansing and reconciling power of Jesus' sacrifice.

- Shelter Them with His Presence (Strong's G4637): Emphasizes the security and protection found in reconciliation with God.

- Lamb as Shepherd (Strong's G4165): Depicts Jesus' role in guiding and caring for the reconciled believers.

This vision highlights the fulfillment of the hope of glory, where believers find ultimate peace, security, and joy in the presence of God.

The New Jerusalem: A Vision of Future Glory

Key Verses: Revelation 21:1-7

The vision of the new Jerusalem offers a powerful image of the future hope and glory that believers anticipate, where God dwells with His people in perfect harmony.

- Revelation 21:1-7 (NIV): "Then I saw 'a new heaven and a new earth,' for the first heaven and the first earth had passed away, and there was no longer any sea. I saw the Holy City, the new Jerusalem, coming down out of heaven from God, prepared as a bride beautifully dressed for her husband.

And I heard a loud voice from the throne saying, 'Look! God's dwelling place is now among the people, and he will dwell with them. They will be his people, and God himself will be with them and be their God. He will wipe every tear from their eyes. There will be no more death or mourning or crying or pain, for the old order of things has passed away.' He who was seated on the throne said, 'I am making everything new!' Then he said, 'Write this down, for these words are trustworthy and true.'"

Expository Insights:

- New Heaven and New Earth (Strong's G2537 and G1093): Signify the complete renewal and restoration of creation, reflecting the ultimate fulfillment of the hope of glory.

- New Jerusalem (Strong's G2419): Represents the redeemed community of God's people, united and glorified in Christ.

- God's Dwelling Place (Strong's G4637): Emphasizes the intimate and eternal relationship between God and His people.

This vision affirms the ultimate fulfillment of the hope of glory, where believers experience eternal life, free from pain and sorrow, in the presence of God.

The Eternal Reign of Christ

Key Verses: Revelation 22:1-5

The vision of the eternal reign of Christ highlights the final and complete realization of the hope of glory, where believers enjoy everlasting life and fellowship with God.

- Revelation 22:1-5 (NIV): "Then the angel showed me the river of the water of life, as clear as crystal, flowing from the throne of God and of the Lamb down the middle of the great street of the city. On each side of the river stood the tree of life, bearing twelve crops of fruit, yielding its fruit every month. And the leaves of the tree are for the healing of the nations. No longer will there be any curse. The throne of God and of the Lamb will be in the city, and his servants will serve him. They will see his face, and his name will be on their foreheads. There will be no more night. They will not need the light of a lamp or the light of the sun, for the Lord God will give them light. And they will reign for ever and ever."

Expository Insights:

- River of the Water of Life (Strong's G5204): Symbolizes the eternal life and sustenance provided by Christ.

- Tree of Life (Strong's G3586 and G2222): Represents the fullness of life and healing available through Christ.

- Throne of God and of the Lamb (Strong's G2362 and G721): Emphasizes the unified and eternal reign of God and Jesus.

This passage affirms the eternal and complete realization of the hope of glory, where believers enjoy everlasting life and fellowship with God in a renewed creation.

Practical Implications of the Hope of Glory

1. Assured Future: Understanding the hope of glory provides believers with assurance and confidence in their future with God.

2. Transformative Living: Embracing the hope of glory inspires believers to live transformed lives, reflecting the character of Christ and embodying His love and grace.

3. Perseverance in Trials: The promise of future glory encourages believers to persevere through trials and sufferings, knowing that their ultimate reward is secure.

4. Unity with God and Others: The vision of the new Jerusalem emphasizes the intimate and eternal relationship believers have with God and with one another, encouraging them to live in harmony and unity.

5. Eternal Perspective: Embracing the hope of glory shifts believers' focus from temporal concerns to the eternal

reality of God's kingdom, inspiring them to live with purpose and anticipation of the renewed creation.

Conclusion

The Book of Revelation vividly portrays the theme of the hope of glory through powerful imagery and declarations. From the vision of the glorified Christ to the multitude before the throne, and from the new Jerusalem to the eternal reign of Christ, Revelation affirms the profound truth of the future hope and glory that believers anticipate through their union with Christ. As we reflect on these truths, we are encouraged to embrace the assurance, transformative power, perseverance, unity, and eternal perspective offered by the hope of glory. Recognizing the significance of this hope transforms our understanding of our relationship with God and our place in His eternal kingdom, grounding us in His eternal purpose and love.

LIVING IN THE FULLNESS OF CHRIST

Embrace the Supremacy of Christ

Living in the fullness of Christ begins with acknowledging and embracing His supremacy. Jesus' preeminence, authority, and divinity are foundational truths that transform our understanding of who He is and how we relate to Him.

- Colossians 1:18 (NIV): "And he is the head of the body, the church; he is the beginning and the firstborn from among the dead, so that in everything he might have the supremacy."

- Revelation 1:17-18 (NIV): "When I saw him, I fell at his feet as though dead. Then he placed his right hand on me and said: 'Do not be afraid. I am the First and the Last. I am the Living One; I was dead, and now look, I am alive for ever and ever! And I hold the keys of death and Hades.'"

By recognizing Jesus' supreme authority, we are called to live lives of worship, obedience, and devotion. His divine nature and eternal reign compel us to submit to His will and trust in His perfect plan.

Walk in New Life

The resurrection of Jesus offers believers a new life, characterized by a focus on heavenly things and a transformation that reflects our hidden life in Christ.

- Colossians 3:1-4 (NIV): "Since, then, you have been raised with Christ, set your hearts on things above, where Christ is, seated at the right hand of God. Set your minds on things above, not on earthly things. For you died, and your life is now hidden with Christ in God. When Christ, who is your life, appears, then you also will appear with him in glory."

- Revelation 21:1-4 (NIV): "Then I saw 'a new heaven and a new earth,' for the first heaven and the first earth had passed away, and there was no longer any sea. I saw the Holy City, the new Jerusalem, coming down out of heaven from God, prepared as a bride beautifully dressed for her husband.

And I heard a loud voice from the throne saying, 'Look! God's dwelling place is now among the people, and he will dwell with them. They will be his people, and God himself will be with them and be their God. He will wipe every tear from their eyes. There will be no more death or mourning or crying or pain, for the old order of things has passed away.'"

Walking in this new life involves daily renewal and transformation, setting our hearts and minds on heavenly realities and living out our identity in Christ.

Experience Reconciliation and Peace

Through Jesus' sacrificial death on the cross, we have been offered reconciliation with God and the peace that surpasses all understanding.

- Colossians 1:19-20 (NIV): "For God was pleased to have all his fullness dwell in him, and through him to reconcile to himself all things, whether things on earth or things in heaven, by making peace through his blood, shed on the cross."

- Revelation 7:9-17 (NIV): "After this I looked, and there before me was a great multitude that no one could count, from every nation, tribe, people and language, standing before the throne and before the Lamb. They were wearing white robes and were holding palm branches in their hands.

And they cried out in a loud voice: 'Salvation belongs to our God, who sits on the throne, and to the Lamb.'"

This peace is not just an absence of conflict but a deep-seated tranquility that comes from being reconciled to God. Embracing this reconciliation allows us to live in harmony with God and others, reflecting the peace of Christ in our lives.

Hope of Glory

The indwelling presence of Christ in believers offers the hope of future glory, a confident assurance of eternal life with Him.

- Colossians 1:26-27 (NIV): "The mystery that has been kept hidden for ages and generations, but is now disclosed to the Lord's people. To them God has chosen to make known among the Gentiles the glorious riches of this mystery, which is Christ in you, the hope of glory."

- Revelation 22:1-5 (NIV): "Then the angel showed me the river of the water of life, as clear as crystal, flowing from the throne of God and of the Lamb down the middle of the great street of the city. On each side of the river stood the tree of life, bearing twelve crops of fruit, yielding its fruit every month. And the leaves of the tree are for the healing of the nations. No longer will there be any curse. The throne of God and of the Lamb will be in the city, and his servants will serve him. They will see his face, and his name will be on their foreheads. There will be no more night. They will not need the light of a lamp or the light of the sun, for the Lord God will give them light. And they will reign for ever and ever."

This hope of glory encourages us to persevere through trials and challenges, knowing that our ultimate reward is eternal life with Christ in His glorious presence.

Conclusion

Living in the fullness of Christ encompasses embracing His supremacy, walking in the new life He offers, experiencing His reconciliation and peace, and holding onto the hope of future glory. The Book of Revelation vividly portrays these truths through powerful imagery and declarations, reminding us of the profound reality of Christ in us and the eternal hope we possess.

As we internalize these truths, we are called to live transformed lives, reflecting the character of Christ and embodying His love and grace. Our focus shifts from temporal concerns to the eternal promises of God, inspiring us to live with purpose, perseverance, and anticipation of the renewed creation. Recognizing the significance of these truths transforms our understanding of our relationship with God and our place in His eternal kingdom, grounding us in His eternal purpose and love.

PRACTICAL APPLICATION

DAILY DEVOTION

Commit to Daily Prayer and Study of Scripture:

To live in the fullness of Christ, it is essential to cultivate a daily habit of prayer and Scripture study. This practice deepens our understanding of Jesus and strengthens our relationship with Him.

- Psalm 119:105 (NIV): "Your word is a lamp for my feet, a light on my path."

- Matthew 6:6 (NIV): "But when you pray, go into your room, close the door and pray to your Father, who is unseen. Then your Father, who sees what is done in secret, will reward you."

By dedicating time each day to connect with God through prayer and His Word, we invite His presence and guidance into our lives, allowing us to grow spiritually and align our hearts with His will.

Community Worship

Engage with the Church Community:

Recognizing Jesus as the head of the church, we are called to actively participate in collective worship and service within the church community.

- Hebrews 10:24-25 (NIV): "And let us consider how we may spur one another on toward love and good deeds, not giving up meeting together, as some are in the habit of doing, but encouraging one another—and all the more as you see the Day approaching."

- Ephesians 4:15-16 (NIV): "Instead, speaking the truth in love, we will grow to become in every respect the mature body of him who is the head, that is, Christ. From him the whole body, joined and held together by every supporting ligament, grows and builds itself up in love, as each part does its work."

Engaging in community worship and service not only strengthens our faith but also fosters unity and mutual encouragement within the body of Christ. It is through collective worship that we experience the fullness of Christ's presence and grow together in love and faith.

Sharing the Mystery

Share the Hope and Mystery of Christ in You:

As believers, we are entrusted with the glorious riches of the mystery of Christ in us, the hope of glory. We are called to share this hope with others, living out the gospel in our everyday interactions.

- 1 Peter 3:15 (NIV): "But in your hearts revere Christ as Lord. Always be prepared to give an answer to everyone who asks you to give the reason for the hope that you have. But do this with gentleness and respect."

- Colossians 4:5-6 (NIV): "Be wise in the way you act toward outsiders; make the most of every opportunity. Let your conversation be always full of grace, seasoned with salt, so that you may know how to answer everyone."

Sharing the hope and mystery of Christ involves both our words and actions. By living out the gospel through acts of kindness, love, and integrity, we demonstrate the transformative power of Christ in our lives and invite others to experience His grace and truth.

Conclusion

Embracing the practical applications of daily devotion, community worship, and sharing the mystery of Christ enables us to live in the fullness of Christ. These practices not only deepen our relationship with Jesus but also help us reflect His love and grace to the world around us. As we commit to these disciplines, we are continually transformed into His likeness, living out the hope and glory that comes from Christ dwelling in us.